# Hands-On Chatbot Development with Alexa Skills and Amazon Lex

Create custom conversational and voice interfaces for your Amazon Echo devices and web platforms

**Sam Williams**

**BIRMINGHAM - MUMBAI**

# Hands-On Chatbot Development with Alexa Skills and Amazon Lex

Copyright © 2018 Packt Publishing

**Commissioning Editor:** Kunal Chaudhari
**Acquisition Editor:** Divya Poojari
**Content Development Editor:** Chris D'cruz
**Technical Editor:** Sneha Hanchate
**Copy Editor:** SAFIS
**Project Coordinator:** Namrata Swetta
**Proofreader:** Safis Editing
**Indexer:** Aishwarya Gangawane
**Graphics:** Jisha Chirayil
**Production Coordinator:** Shraddha Falebhai

First published: October 2016

Production reference: 1270918

Published by Packt Publishing Ltd.
Livery Place
35 Livery Street
Birmingham
B3 2PB, UK.

ISBN 978-1-78899-348-7

www.packtpub.com

mapt.io

Mapt is an online digital library that gives you full access to over 5,000 books and videos, as well as industry leading tools to help you plan your personal development and advance your career. For more information, please visit our website.

# Why subscribe?

- Spend less time learning and more time coding with practical eBooks and Videos from over 4,000 industry professionals

- Improve your learning with Skill Plans built especially for you

- Get a free eBook or video every month

- Mapt is fully searchable

- Copy and paste, print, and bookmark content

# Packt.com

Did you know that Packt offers eBook versions of every book published, with PDF and ePub files available? You can upgrade to the eBook version at www.packt.com and as a print book customer, you are entitled to a discount on the eBook copy. Get in touch with us at customercare@packt.com for more details.

At www.packt.com, you can also read a collection of free technical articles, sign up for a range of free newsletters, and receive exclusive discounts and offers on Packt books and eBooks.

# Contributors

## About the author

**Sam Williams** qualified with an aerospace engineering master's degree, then became a self-taught software developer while holding down his first job. While traveling, he started to write articles about the tech he was learning about and accrued an audience of readers on Medium and freeCodeCamp.

Currently, Sam works as a lead chatbot developer for the SmartAgent team at MissionLabs, building custom systems for large retailers. His role ensures that he is working with the newest chatbot technologies and is constantly pushing their capabilities.

*I want to thank Walter Quesada for his excellent technical feedback throughout the development of this book and Alice Oberacker for her editorial help.*

# About the reviewer

**Walter Quesada** is a software engineer and technologist with over 20 years' experience architecting and developing solutions for companies of all sizes. He currently serves as the conversational systems lead at the PwC Applied Research Lab, where he focuses on creating a more conversational future with voice and chatbots. He is also an Amazon Alexa Champion, an O'Reilly author with a book titled *Programming Voice Interfaces*, as well as being a Pluralsight instructor with two courses, *Developing Alexa Skills for Amazon Echo* and *Creating Voice and Chatbots that Work Everywhere*.

# Packt is searching for authors like you

If you're interested in becoming an author for Packt, please visit `authors.packtpub.com` and apply today. We have worked with thousands of developers and tech professionals, just like you, to help them share their insight with the global tech community. You can make a general application, apply for a specific hot topic that we are recruiting an author for, or submit your own idea.

# Table of Contents

# Preface

Chatbots are becoming more and more common in everyday life, with Alexa currently being in 16% of households and over 100,000 Facebook chatbots. Chatbots provide a way to interact with technology that is a lot more natural for people, through conversation.

In this book, we'll learn how to build our own voice and text-based chatbots using Amazon Alexa and Lex. These platforms allow us to use very powerful technology to understand what the users are saying. We also learn about the design process when creating a chatbot and how we can provide a great experience for our users.

## Who this book is for

This book is for anyone who wants to be able to build Alexa Skills or Lex chatbots. Whether you want to build them for personal projects or as part of your job, this book will give you all the tools you need. You'll be able to take an idea, build the conversation flow diagrams, test them with user stories, and then build your Alexa Skill or Lex chatbot.

## What this book covers

Chapter 1, *Understanding Chatbots*, starts by explaining the concepts involved in building a conversational interface. We will learn how to start with an example user conversation and build flow diagrams to visualize the path that the user takes with the chatbot. The chapter will then discuss the types of chatbots and will introduce us to voice skills for Amazon Alexa and text-based chatbots for Amazon Lex.

Chapter 2, *Getting Started with AWS and Amazon CLI*, teaches us about AWS Lambdas and how these serverless functions can be built and tested in the browser. After building our first Lambda, we discuss three different ways to build and deploy them, comparing the merits and limits of each. To create the most powerful development environment possible, we use `aws-cli` to build a script that allows us to deploy Lambdas from our local development environment.

Chapter 3, *Creating Your First Alexa Skill,* introduces us to the Alexa Skills Kit and has us build our first Alexa Skill. We learn about how to build a Lambda to handle our users' requests and return the response that we want to send to the user. To create a more realistic situation, we create a skill that suggests a car for the user, based on a series of questions. We use the flow design process discussed in Chapter 1, *Understanding Chatbots,* to map out our users' interactions with our skill before creating the intents. The Lambdas that we use also increase in complexity with *slot eliciting* and with the inclusion of data that is stored in S3.

Chapter 4, *Connecting Your Alexa Skills to External APIs,* takes our Alexa skills to a new level of functionality by accessing external APIs. API access can provide massive amounts of functionality to your chatbots, but it needs to be done correctly. We'll learn about two of the best ways to handle errors and use them to build a weather skill.

Chapter 5, *Building Your First Amazon Lex Chatbot,* moves the focus onto Amazon Lex chatbots. The concepts and components are similar to those we used to build our Alexa skills, so we only need a quick refresher before building our first Lex chatbot. While Lex and Alexa are similar, we quickly see how there are some key differences in the way that the intents are handled. To create a more realistic project, we build an FAQ chatbot. This Lex chatbot takes advantage of the intent handling by triggering one of three Lambdas, based on the intent that was hit. These Lambdas access the responses from S3 and reply using a LexResponses class, which we will build.

Chapter 6, *Connecting a Lex Bot to DynamoDB,* introduces us to DynamoDB databases and how we can use them to store information about the users' interactions. We use this to build ourselves a shopping chatbot that stores a user's cart, even allowing them to save their cart for later. The complexity of the flows for this chatbot is a lot closer to what you would expect from a real project, and that is reflected in the amount of code.

Chapter 7, *Publishing Your Chatbot to Facebook, Slack, Twilio, and HTTP,* teaches us how we can publish our chatbots and integrate them into platforms, including Facebook and Slack. We use Amazon Lex's built-in integration tools to make this process as easy as possible. Next, we build an API endpoint, using API Gateway and Lambdas, so that we can develop integrations for other services. We use this API ourselves to create our own front-end interface, which we could integrate into other websites.

Chapter 8, *Improving User Experience for Your Bots,* discusses a few ways to make the experiences of your users more enjoyable. This covers creating and sending cards in Lex conversations and using *search query* slot types in Alexa skills. Cards provide the user with a much more visual interaction, while *search query* slots allow a user to search for a much wider range of values that we could allow with a custom or built-in slot type.

Chapter 9, *Review and Continued Development*, gives us a few pointers on the directions we can go to continue developing our chatbot skills. There are separate pieces of advice for people who prefer Alexa, and those who want to pursue more Lex skills, as well as a set of skills that will improve your abilities with both chatbot platforms. After this, we discuss the future of chatbots, where they are going, and what needs to happen before they become truly integrated into our daily lives.

# To get the most out of this book

Here is a list of things that you should have to make the most out of this book. You can complete this book without the second or third items, but lacking them will make the process harder:

- Knowledge of at least one high-level programming language supported by AWS, but ideally JavaScript
- Basic experience using command-line tools for Linux or macOS
- A basic understanding of AWS services is helpful, but not required

# Download the example code files

You can download the example code files for this book from your account at www.packt.com. If you purchased this book elsewhere, you can visit www.packt.com/support and register to have the files emailed directly to you.

You can download the code files by following these steps:

1. Log in or register at www.packt.com.
2. Select the **SUPPORT** tab.
3. Click on **Code Downloads & Errata**.
4. Enter the name of the book in the **Search** box and follow the onscreen instructions.

Once the file is downloaded, please make sure that you unzip or extract the folder using the latest version of:

- WinRAR/7-Zip for Windows
- Zipeg/iZip/UnRarX for Mac
- 7-Zip/PeaZip for Linux

The code bundle for the book is also hosted on GitHub
at https://github.com/PacktPublishing/Hands-On-Chatbot-Development-with-Alexa-Skills-and-Amazon-Lex. In case there's an update to the code, it will be updated on the existing GitHub repository.

We also have other code bundles from our rich catalog of books and videos available at https://github.com/PacktPublishing/. Check them out!

# Download the color images

We also provide a PDF file that has color images of the screenshots/diagrams used in this book. You can download it here: https://www.packtpub.com/sites/default/files/downloads/9781788993487_ColorImages.pdf.

# Conventions used

There are a number of text conventions used throughout this book.

CodeInText: Indicates code in text, database table names, folder names, filenames, file extensions, pathnames, dummy URLs, user input, and Twitter handles. Here is an example: "Mount the downloaded WebStorm-10*.dmg disk image file as another disk in your system."

A block of code is set as follows:

```
html, body, #map {
    height: 100%;
    margin: 0;
    padding: 0
}
```

When we wish to draw your attention to a particular part of a code block, the relevant lines or items are set in bold:

```
[default]
exten => s,1,Dial(Zap/1|30)
exten => s,2,Voicemail(u100)
exten => s,102,Voicemail(b100)
exten => i,1,Voicemail(s0)
```

Any command-line input or output is written as follows:

```
$ mkdir css
$ cd css
```

**Bold**: Indicates a new term, an important word, or words that you see onscreen. For example, words in menus or dialogue boxes appear in the text like this. Here is an example: "Select **System info** from the **Administration** panel."

Warnings or important notes appear like this.

Tips and tricks appear like this.

# Get in touch

Feedback from our readers is always welcome.

**General feedback**: If you have questions about any aspect of this book, mention the book title in the subject of your message and email us at customercare@packtpub.com.

**Errata**: Although we have taken every care to ensure the accuracy of our content, mistakes do happen. If you have found a mistake in this book, we would be grateful if you would report this to us. Please visit www.packt.com/submit-errata, selecting your book, clicking on the Errata Submission Form link, and entering the details.

**Piracy**: If you come across any illegal copies of our works in any form on the Internet, we would be grateful if you would provide us with the location address or website name. Please contact us at copyright@packt.com with a link to the material.

**If you are interested in becoming an author**: If there is a topic that you have expertise in and you are interested in either writing or contributing to a book, please visit authors.packtpub.com.

# Reviews

Once you have read and used this book, why not leave a review on the site that you purchased it from? Potential readers can then see and use your unbiased opinion to make purchase decisions, we at Packt can understand what you think about our products, and our authors can see your feedback on their book. Thank you!

For more information about Packt, please visit packt.com.

# 1
# Understanding Chatbots

To create successful chatbots using Alexa or Lex, you first need to understand the components that make up a chatbot. These parts can then be used to create conversation diagrams and flow diagrams, helping visualize the user's path through the conversation. Being able to have this map for the user's conversation makes building chatbots far easier and quicker.

Toward the end of the chapter, we will also introduce Alexa and Lex and have a look at their similarities and differences. We'll also have a quick look at some of the use cases for each of them.

The chapter will explain the following topics:

- Introducing chatbots
- Designing conversation flow diagrams
- Best practices
- Amazon Alexa and Amazon Lex

## What are chatbots?

Chatbots are a new way to interact with a user in a more human way, through conversation. This is vastly different from existing methods, which provide minimal interaction or personalization.

Chatbots can be either voice or text-based interactions, allowing them to be integrated into existing websites and apps or used in phone calls and virtual assistants.

They have recently been put in the spotlight with products such as Amazon Echo and Google Home, as well as an enormous number of Facebook Messenger chatbots. These advances in technology allow you to check the weather or order a pizza without looking at a screen, or get personalized information without having to wait to talk to a call center.

# What makes up a chatbot?

A chatbot is very different in the way that it interacts with a user, and therefore how it works is also very different. There are three main components of a chatbot: **intents**, **slots**, and **utterances**.

## Intents

Intents are the most important part of a chatbot. They are the tasks or conversations that the chatbot can process. They are called intents because they are the things that the user intends to do.

Intents can vary in complexity from very simple to extremely complicated. A basic intent may just be `SayHello`, which just says "Hi" to the user. A more complex intent may be booking a holiday, choosing and buying a pair of shoes, or ordering a pizza. They can be designed to be as elaborate as your imagination allows.

They are started or triggered when the user says one of the **sample utterances**. The sample utterances are a list of words or phrases that the user might say when they are trying to start an intent. Each intent can have lots of sample utterances. In the `SayHello` example, they might be "Hello chatbot", "Hey there chatbot", or just "Hi".

## Slots

To allow the chatbot to be really useful, it has to be able to gather details about what the user is asking for. If you are wanting to order a pizza, the chatbot needs to know what toppings you want, what style of base you want, and where you want it delivered to. This information is collected and stored in slots.

Slots are designed to only accept certain types of information. If you were trying to find out whether they wanted a large, medium, or small pizza, it wouldn't be very useful if they could enter any random information. Defining the information that can be stored in a certain slot is called creating a **slot type**.

To make use of the information gathered in the slots, they can be accessed in the next stage of the chatbot logic. This could be as simple as saying "You have ordered a *large Hawaiian* pizza", where the size and topping are exactly what the user previously ordered.

## Utterances

An utterance is a word or phrase that has been said. This is key to chatbots as this is how a user interacts with the chatbot.

These utterances can trigger which intent the user is trying to access and they can also be used to get the exact information needed to fill the slots.

# Designing conversation flows

Now that we understand the components that make up a chatbot, we can start to design the conversations that we want our chatbot to handle. Designing conversations now makes it a lot easier to visualize how the chatbot will work, making it easier and quicker to build. Designing conversations in this way makes them easy to understand, making it a great tool for creating chatbots with people who can't code.

This design method will work for voice or text chatbots; just imagine the textboxes as speech bubbles.

# Starting with the perfect conversation diagram

Everything has to start somewhere, so it may as well be perfect. The aim of this stage is to have a basic conversation diagram that we will later expand into a detailed flow diagram.

To do this, you need to think about what the perfect conversation with your user would be. Start by writing down what the user will say and how the bot will respond. This is an example of ordering a pizza:

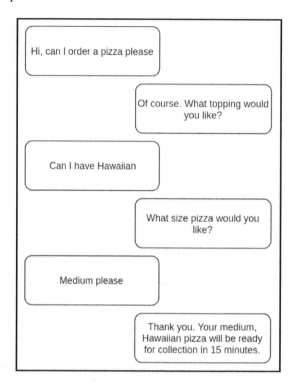

Ordering pizza conversation

This can be done in lots of ways: with flow diagram software, using two phones or two messaging accounts, or simply with pen and paper. The aim is just to understand how the chatbot is going to be interacting with the user and what utterances the user is likely to say.

# Conversation flow diagrams

Now that you have a basic conversation diagram, we need to make it into a flow diagram. A flow diagram is different from a conversation diagram in a few key ways:

- Each part of a flow diagram has its own symbol, making it easy to understand what is happening at each stage.
- A flow diagram contain more than just the conversation. It also describes the logic, information, and processes that take place behind the scenes.

- Flow diagrams aren't linear. This means that they can describe lots of conversations where the user says different things.

To properly describe our chatbots, we need to have a symbol for each of the parts of the conversation. To start with, we are going to be using six, but we can add more symbols later on:

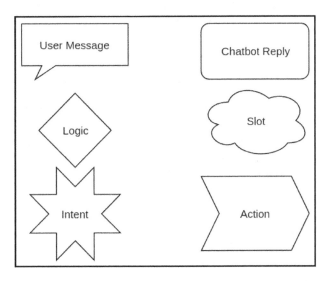

Flow diagram symbols

To create our flow diagrams, we'll be using flow diagram software. There are a couple of reasons we want to use flow diagram software instead of a normal document or even creating them by hand:

- They are easily editable. We are going to be changing the stages of the conversational flow and the text of utterances and replies as we work through this book. Having to redraw the diagram every time you make a change would be very time-consuming.
- It's the easiest way to make flow diagrams. The symbols snap into place and are easy to edit and modify. Doing flow diagrams in Word would be far more time-consuming.

In all of the examples throughout this book, we'll be using `www.draw.io`, but if you have a different flow diagram software that you prefer then that will work too. We use draw.io as it's free, online, and is very easy to use.

# Creating a conversation flow diagram

Now that we know the parts of a conversation flow diagram, let's create one. We'll use the same pizza order conversation that we used earlier.

Start at the very beginning of the conversation. Create a symbol for the user's first utterance. This first message from the user is a really important one as it will trigger an intent:

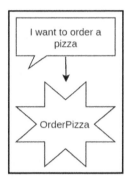

Utterance triggering an intent

Now that the OrderPizza intent has been triggered, our chatbot can start asking the user about the pizza they want to order. We'll start by asking what topping they want and they reply with "Hawaiian":

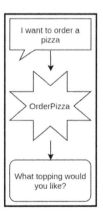

Starting the intent

Later on, we want to remember that they chose Hawaiian as their topping so we need to store this as a slot. We store the information against a slot name, so in this case, it will be **topping = Hawaiian**. As well as storing the slot, we need to carry on the conversation, asking them what size of pizza they want:

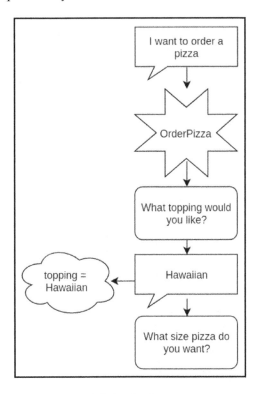

Storing a slot value

With the response from the user, we store the size in a slot and proceed to the next stage. We repeat the question, answer, slot process for the size of pizza the user wants.

Now that we have all of the information that we need, we need to tell the pizzeria that someone has ordered a medium Hawaiian pizza. For this, we'll use the action symbol and make sure to include the slots that are required. When we include slot information into anything, it is normal to write it as the slot name wrapped in curly braces.

As well as telling the pizzeria about the order, we need to let the user know that their order has been placed and tell them when to collect it. Again, we use the slot name wrapped in curly braces to customize the message with slot information:

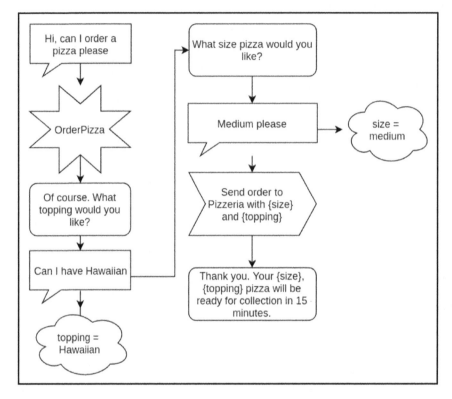

Full pizza ordering flow diagram

# User stories

User stories are a vital tool in the design and testing of chatbots. They are stories about fictional users, what they want, and how they will interact with your bot. When we create a user story, it needs to be as close to a real user as possible. They should be based on a real user or the type of user that would be using your chatbot. If you have existing customers that you are wanting to target your chatbot toward then you can create data-driven user stories.

To create a user story, start by describing the user and why they are talking with your bot. Examples of the pizza ordering bot might be the following:

- Chris, a 23-year-old joiner. Wants to order a pizza on his phone so he can pick it up on the way home from work.
- Claire, a 35-year-old bank manager. Ordering a pizza using Alexa while she watches TV.

The user descriptions don't have to be very long or complicated, but they have to represent the kind of users the bot will get.

For each user, go through the flow diagram pretending that the bot is talking to that user. The aim of this is to test your flow diagram before we start building the bot. If you find that the conversation doesn't work for a certain part of the flow diagram, changing it now will save you time later on.

For simple examples like this pizza order, there won't be a big difference between all of the conversations, but user stories will become more important as we create more complicated flow diagrams.

# Best practices

Anyone can make a chatbot. With a bit of practice, you can build a simple bot in a few hours. The problem with building bots like this is that, as they grow in scope and complexity, they can very easily become unmanageable. Simple changes can result in hours or even days of bug fixing and it can ruin the joy you get when you finally get the chatbot working.

To avoid the horror of working with a disorganized and complex chatbot, there are a few best practices. Following these will reduce your headache later on and allow you to quickly and easily add new features.

# Handling errors

Throughout a user's conversation with a chatbot, there are a lot of points where errors can occur. Errors can occur when an utterance isn't understood, an API returns an error or when there is a mistake in the developer's code. Each of these needs to be caught and dealt with properly. We'll cover how to use `try/catch` and the `to()` method to catch these errors in `Chapter 4`, *Connecting Your Alexa Skill to External APIs*.

# Missed utterances

The most common error will be when utterances aren't understood or aren't what the chatbot expected. This can be because the user typed something incorrectly, misspelled a word, or just typed a response you hadn't thought of. Alexa and Lex both use **natural language understanding** (**NLU**) to try to reduce the errors from misspelling and varied responses but they aren't perfect.

Because not understanding the user's utterance is such a common error, both Lex and Alexa also have systems to handle them. This involves a failure phrase that can be sent to the user when the chatbot doesn't understand what the user just said. Make sure that this is set up properly and that you are asking the user to try again or to choose a different option:

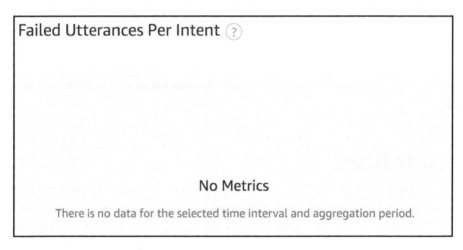

Failed utterances

Alexa and Lex also have a feature that stores all of the times that it couldn't understand an utterance. Using this list, you can add more sample utterances to help the chatbot understand more. Doing this regularly can give a massive boost to your user satisfaction, as well as helping you understand how your users interact with your bot.

# External APIs

Every time you deal with anything outside of your code, there is a risk that it will error. This might be a third-party API, your own API, or simply a query to a database. You should always write these requests so that if the request returns an error, you fully deal with it. This means logging what the error was and where it took place and making sure that the chatbot still works when an error occurs.

Making sure that the chatbot still works when an error occurs is really important. [...]
wants to talk to a chatbot that just stops talking to you halfway through the conve[...]
To make sure this doesn't happen, you have three options: create error messages f[...]
external call you make, let all errors flow down to a very low-level error handler that sends
a generic *We had an error* message, or a combination of the two. The idea would be using
custom messages for every error that could happen but as your chatbot becomes larger and
more complicated, that can become very time-consuming.

An effective method for dealing with the errors is to create a low-level error handler that
passes a generic error message unless a specific error message is provided. This gives you
the flexibility to let the user know exactly what went wrong when it matters but saves you
having to create lots of similar error messages:

```
try {
    let result = AccessPeopleAPI();
    if (result === null || typeof result !== 'number'){
        throw 'I've failed to get the number of people';
    }
    return 'We have ' + result + ' people in the building';
} catch (error) {
    console.log(error || 'The system has had an error');
    return error || "Unfortunately I've had an error";
}
```

## Errors in your code

No developer wants to admit there are bugs in their code, but if you create more than a
simple chatbot, there probably will be. There are different ways to approach this problem,
from writing tests for every function, to thorough end-to-end testing, to wrapping
everything in a `try/catch`. This book will let you decide how you want to deal with these
errors, but expecting your code to be error-free is a very dangerous path.

No matter how you want to stop errors getting into your code, you need to deal with them
when you get them. This is where having a low-level error handler can also be of use. You
can use that to catch errors that have occurred in your code the same way that you deal
with errors from external APIs.

## Tone of voice

One of the best things about chatbots is the fact that they are conversational and feel more
human. Because of this, you need to give your bot a personality and you need to tailor that
personality to suit the purpose of the chatbot and the users who will be interacting with it.

Having a banking chatbot that uses slang might make the users trust the chatbot less, whereas having a clothing sales chatbot that uses lots of very formal or old-fashioned language might be just as off-putting.

Try to design the language that the chatbot uses to be in line with your brand persona. If you don't have a brand persona then you can build one by interviewing your staff and customers. Use these interviews to create a persona (similar to a user story) that relates closely to your customers.

# Identifying suitable use cases

Chatbots are awesome! Being able to create a new way for users to interact is such a great feeling that you want to make a chatbot for everything. Unfortunately, chatbots aren't suited to every situation and some things need to be carefully thought through before being implemented. You need to think about whether users would want to talk about certain things with a chatbot, as well as how the chatbot will be communicating back.

Thinking about the way that the bot will be communicating is particularly important for voice-based chatbots, as everything that the chatbot says will be sent through speakers for everyone around to hear. This could end badly for a chatbot that accesses your bank information, reads your emails, or deals with any other personal information. When designing your Alexa conversations, ask yourself whether you'd want Alexa telling all of your friends and colleagues about your results from your doctor's appointment or reading out an email from your partner about what they had planned for that evening.

# Designing the information for the delivery method

As the method of information delivery is very different from existing methods (emails, websites, and printed media), you also need to think about what it will be like for the user. For example, when creating a newspaper chatbot, having Alexa read the whole paper for 15 minutes or Lex send a huge chunk of text might not be very user-friendly. Instead, you could break down the information into smaller chunks, or give a brief overview of the information.

There can be a fine line between a chatbot that provides the user with great information and one that talks too much. Make sure that the amount of information is designed in a way that is suited to the end delivery method.

# Amazon Alexa and Lex

Alexa and Lex are a pair of tools built by Amazon to change the way that users interact with technology. They are platforms that allow developers to create immensely powerful conversational interfaces without having to study deep learning, natural language processing, or speech recognition.

They are part of the **Amazon Web Services** (**AWS**) group and therefore work brilliantly alongside the rest of the services, making the development process smoother and more consistent.

The main difference between Alexa and Lex is that the Alexa platform allows developers to create skills for Alexa-enabled devices, whereas Lex allows developers to create generic text or voice-based chatbots.

# Amazon Alexa

Amazon Alexa is a voice-based chatbot that is the brains behind the Echo family of products from Amazon. Users can customize their Echo experience by adding **skills** to their Alexa account in a similar way to how you add apps onto a smartphone. These skills can be downloaded from the Alexa Skills Store and there are thousands to choose from.

Similar to apps, each of these skills has been designed to perform a single task, whether that's to talk you through a recipe to cook, guide you through your morning workout, or just to tell you jokes.

Alexa was released in November 2014 and has become increasingly popular. By the end of 2017, Amazon had sold tens of millions of Alexa-connected devices. This has resulted in Alexa devices securing 55% of the market for virtual assistants by February 2018.

# Amazon Lex

Amazon Lex is a chatbot service that allows developers to create either text- or voice-based chatbots, utilizing the incredible power of the deep learning, natural language understanding, and speech recognition that Amazon has developed. Lex differs from Alexa in that it can be integrated into different devices and services.

Lex is most commonly used as a text-based chatbot. There are loads of different ways that users interact with text-based chats, and Lex can integrate with a lot of them. Developers can create Facebook Messenger bots, Slack bots, Kik bots, and Twilio texting bots through integrations built into the Lex platform.

Lex can also be triggered through the AWS-SDK, meaning that it can be put behind an endpoint. This means that developers can set up a system where they post messages to an API and get back the response from Lex. This gives you the flexibility to send messages to Lex from almost any system. This can be used to create a chat window inside a website, create a chatbot on almost any messaging service, or integrate it with any system that can connect with the internet.

Using Amazon Transcribe for speech recognition, you could create a system very similar to Alexa. This has been used very effectively in call centers, allowing a customer to talk to a virtual service representative instead of just waiting until a human service representative is available. This means that a lot of callers can get the information that they need without talking to a human. This has the dual effect of reducing the time to get an answer if the bot can solve your problem, and reducing the number of people going through to the call center, reducing call wait times.

# Summary

In this chapter, we've learned about the components of chatbots—intents, slots, and utterances—and the role that each of them plays.

Next, we learned how to design conversation flows, starting with an ideal conversation and converting it into a conversation flow diagram. Using flowchart software, we created conversation flow diagrams to help visualize how our chatbot will interact with the users.

We talked about the best practices for creating a chatbot, from handling errors to designing your conversations to work well on chatbots, from the tone of voice to good chatbot use cases.

The last part of this chapter introduced Amazon Alexa and Amazon Lex. We learned about the similarities and differences between the two types of chatbot as well as a bit of background into them both.

# Questions

1. What are the three main components of a chatbot?
2. Name two things that Alexa and Amazon Lex have in common.
3. Name two differences between Alexa and Amazon Lex.
4. When designing a conversation flow, where should you start?
5. What does *tone of voice* mean?
6. What are the three main types of errors that can occur in chatbots?

# Getting Started with AWS and Amazon CLI

**2**

**Amazon Web Services** (**AWS**) is the collection of all the tools and services that Amazon provides for developers in the cloud. There is a huge range of services available, from a server hosting to machine learning, from game streaming to digital marketing. Each of these services has been designed to perform one thing really well, but the biggest benefit is how well each of the services works together.

In this chapter, we will create an AWS account and explore the AWS console. Once we've got our account set up we'll learn about Lambda functions, creating one of our own. This will start out as a very simple Lambda, but we'll increase the functionality as we go through the rest of this book.

The next section of this chapter will talk about the different ways in which we can edit Lambdas and the advantages and disadvantages of each method.

The final section will cover how to create an amazing local development environment, using AWS CLI, build scripts, and Git. By the end of this chapter, we'll have a local environment where we can easily deploy our Lambdas without ever having to go onto AWS and we can back up all of our work to remote Git repositories.

This chapter will cover the following:

- Creating and configuring an AWS account
- Creating a Lambda in AWS Console
- Three methods for editing Lambdas
- Creating an amazing local development environment using AWS CLI, build scripts, and Git

# Technical requirements

In this chapter, we'll be creating a few Lambdas as well as creating a build script.

All of the code can be found at `http://bit.ly/chatbot-ch2`.

# Creating an account

To access all of these services you need to create a free AWS developer account. Go to `aws.amazon.com` and click **Create a Free Account**. To create an account you need to follow the sign-up process. The process is very thorough and requires you to enter payment details and receive an automated phone call. This process is to validate that you are a genuine user.

Once you've created your AWS account you can access all of the services through the Amazon Console (`console.aws.amazon.com`). There is a lot of useful information on the console page. **Build a solution** and **Learn to build** are tutorials and information on how to use some of the services.

# Setting your region

For this book, you will need to set your region to **N. Virginia** or **Ireland**. Lex is currently (April 2018) available in those two regions.

AWS has this concept of regions, which are locations around the world where Amazon have their cloud service centers. Each region is separate from all the others for most applications. It is best practice to deploy services to the regions closest to where they'll be used. If your customers are on the west coast of America then choosing **N. California** or **Oregon** would be best, whilst choosing **Ireland** wouldn't be a great choice. Their data would have to go halfway around the world and back each time they use your product.

One other consideration for the regions is that not every region is equal. Some regions have the larger working capacity, while some don't even have all of the services.

# Navigating around AWS

Getting around AWS has been designed to be as easy as possible. At the top of every page is a banner with a link to the console home page, a dropdown with every service available, account and location settings, and a support menu:

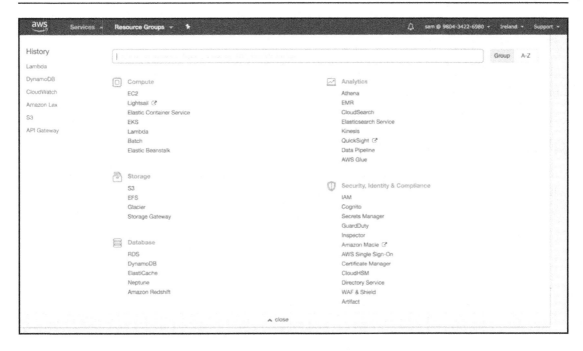

AWS menu and Service dropdown

The link to the home page and the service dropdown are the two options that you'll be using a lot throughout your time in AWS. When you're editing a Lambda and need to check a table name in Dynamo or you're creating an API Gateway for your EC2, you'll be switching between services a lot.

You can also pin your favorite service to your banner using the drawing pin icon. This makes switching between your most used services even quicker.

# Creating a Lambda

AWS Lambda functions are incredible! They're functions that are hosted on AWS that can be triggered in many different ways. Lambda functions are *serverless*, which means that you don't need to run a server to use them. This makes it a lot quicker and easier to set up and use.

One of the best parts of AWS Lambdas is that you only pay for the time the Lambda function is running. Got something that only runs once an hour and only takes two seconds? You'll only be charged for 48 seconds a day! That's insane compared to running a 24/7 AWS EC2 server or your own private server.

Today, we'll create a Lambda function and look at the three best ways to work with the code.

Once you've got your AWS account set up, there are a few ways to create a new Lambda function. We're going to start by using the AWS Console.

# AWS Console

Within the AWS Console, you can find AWS Lambda in **Services** | **Compute** | **Lambda**, which takes you to the Lambda Console:

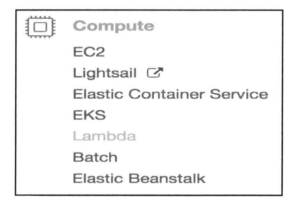

AWS Compute services

This is what you'll see if this is your first Lambda. Click that **Create function** button to start setting up your first function.

You'll end up on the setup page, where you configure some aspects of the function (name, runtime, role). You can create a Lambda from Blueprints or Serverless Application Repos, but in this example, we'll select **Author from scratch**.

# Setting up the Lambda

Enter the name for your function (this must be unique to your user or sub-account), choose your Runtime (We'll use **Node.js 8.10**), and select **Create new role from template(s)**. Give this new role a relevant name, such as `lambdaBasic` or `NoPolicyRol`, and leave **Policy templates** blank. When we create a more complex Lambda, we'll have to create a role with policies and permissions:

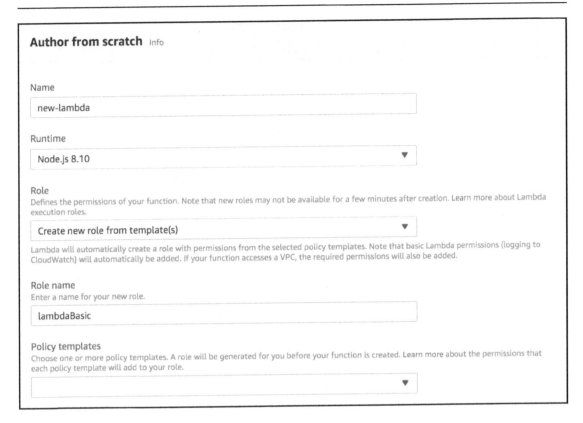

**Author from scratch** Info

Name

new-lambda

Runtime

Node.js 8.10 ▼

Role

Defines the permissions of your function. Note that new roles may not be available for a few minutes after creation. Learn more about Lambda execution roles.

Create new role from template(s) ▼

Lambda will automatically create a role with permissions from the selected policy templates. Note that basic Lambda permissions (logging to CloudWatch) will automatically be added. If your function accesses a VPC, the required permissions will also be added.

Role name

Enter a name for your new role.

lambdaBasic

Policy templates

Choose one or more policy templates. A role will be generated for you before your function is created. Learn more about the permissions that each policy template will add to your role.

▼

New Lambda with a new role

# Writing your Lambda function's code

Once you've created your Lambda you are sent into the function editor within the Lambda Management Console. There is a lot going on this page, but we're focused on the section titled **Function code**.

When you first create a Lambda, it is created with a very basic function already implemented. This is nice as it gives you a starting point to build your function on. As we're using **Node.js 8.10** as our runtime, there will be a single parameter of the event and then we will return our answer.

As a basic example, we'll create a Lambda that takes your name and age and tells you what your maximum heart rate is. This can be done more efficiently than the way we are going to do it, but this is done more as a way to demonstrate some techniques for use within Lambdas.

To start, we will `console.log` out the event and then extract the `name` and `age`. I'm going to use ES6 destructuring but you can also do this using normal variable declaration:

```
exports.handler = async (event) => {
    console.log(event);
    let { name, age } = event;
    // same as => let name = event.name; let age = event.age
    return 'Hello from Lambda!'
};
```

Now that we have the `name` and `age` from the event, we can pass those into a function that converts them into a string:

```
const createString = (name, age) => {
  return `Hi ${name}, you are ${age} years old.`;
};
```

If you haven't seen this sort of string before, they're called **template strings** and they're much neater than previous string concatenation. Backticks start and end the string and you can insert data using `${data}`.

Now we can change `'Hello from Lambda!'` to `createString(name, age)` and our function will return our new string:

```
exports.handler = async (event) => {
    console.log(event);
    let { name, age } = event;
    // same as => let name = event.name; let age = event.age
    return createString(name, age);
};
```

Make sure to save your changes by clicking the bright orange **Save** button in the upper-right corner of your Lambda toolbar:

Lambda toolbar

To test this out, we can click **Test** in the Lambda toolbar.

When we click on **Test**, a **Configure test event** popup opens. We can use this to decide what gets sent to our Lambda in the event payload. Give your test a name and then we can configure our data. For this Lambda it is very simple, just an object with keys of `"name"` and `"age"`. Here's mine:

```
{
    "name": "Sam",
    "age": "24"
}
```

You can set your values to whatever you want and then click **Save** at the bottom of the configuration screen. Now the dropdown to the left of the **Test** button has changed to be your new test name. To run the test, simply click the **Test** button:

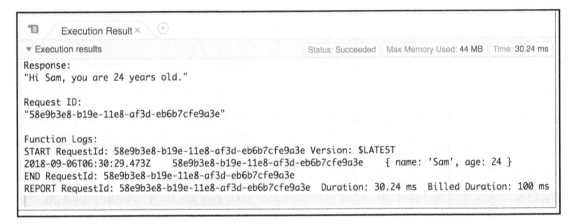

Lambda result

If your response is still `'Hello from Lambda!'`, then make sure you've saved your function and run the test again. As you can see, I got the response of **"Hi Sam, you are 24 years old."**, which is what we expected. As well as the response, we get a **RequestID** and **Function Logs**. Remember when we added that `console.log(event)` to our code? You can now see that the object `{ name: 'Sam', age: '24' }` was logged out. If you want to see more of your logs or logs from previous Lambda calls, they're all stored in CloudWatch. To get to CloudWatch you can either search for it in the services or get there by selecting **Monitoring** at the top of the Lambda Console and then clicking **View logs in CloudWatch**.

There are also some interesting graphs inside **Monitoring** that can tell you a lot about how well your function is working:

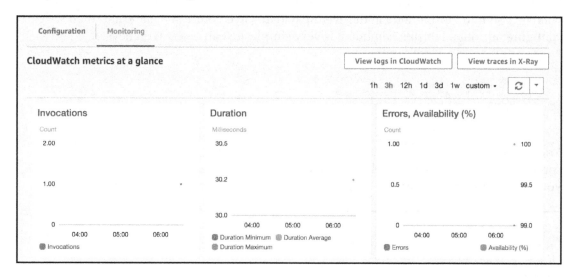

View logs in CloudWatch

Lambda functions can be created in a single file like we have done, but they also work with multiple files. When your Lambda is doing very complex tasks, you can break each section out into its own file to improve organization and readability.

We're going to create a new file called hr.js, and inside we're going to create and export another function. This function is going to calculate your maximum heart rate based on your age. Create the new file by right-clicking in the folder menu and selecting **New File** and call it hr.js. Open up that file and we'll create a calculateHR function:

```
module.exports = {
    calculateHR: (age) => {
        return 220 - age;
    }
}
```

Now, back in our index.js file we need to import our hr.js file and call the calculateHR function:

```
const HR = require('./hr');
exports.handler = async (event) => {
    console.log(event);
    let { name, age } = event;
    return createString(name, age);
```

```
};
const createString = (name, age) => {
  return `Hi ${name}, you are ${age} years old and have a maximum heart rate
of ${HR.calculateHR(age)}.`;
};
```

When we run our last test again, we get a new response of `"Hi Sam, you are 24 years old and have a maximum heart rate of 196."`. This could have been done a lot more effectively, but this was done more to show you some ways that you can write code in Lambda functions.

# Triggering Lambdas

In your first Lambda, the way that we tested it was by triggering it with a test. To make Lambdas useful, we need to be able to trigger it from different places.

In the Lambda Console, near the top, there is a **Designer** section. This section allows you to change how the Lambda interacts with other services and therefore the user. On the left of the section is an **Add triggers** menu with a selection of options. Each of these is a system of services that you can set up to trigger the function. These are not all of the ways to trigger a Lambda and we'll be using other methods in the future.

The most important ones for us are **API Gateway** and **Alexa Skill Kit**, but the other triggers can be very useful for other projects. API Gateway is the way to expose the Lambda to the outside world. You create an API endpoint, and anyone can hit that endpoint and that data will be processed by your Lambda. We'll be creating an API in Chapter 7, *Publishing Your Chatbot to Facebook, Slack, Twilio and HTTP*. The Alexa Skill Kit is a service for building Alexa Skills and these can trigger Lambdas too, and we'll be doing this in the next chapter.

# Methods for working with Lambdas

One of the big advantages of Lambdas is that you can choose how you write and edit them. There are three main ways to do so:

- Lambda Console
- Cloud9
- On your local machine

I'm going to cover all three and discuss the advantages and disadvantages of each of them.

# Method 1 – Lambda Console

This is the way that we have just created our first Lambda function. In the Lambda Console, we have a basic editor. It's based on the Cloud9 IDE and works well for simple Lambda functions.

**The advantages:**

- It's a good editor
- You can access it from any computer through your AWS Console

**The disadvantages:**

- It doesn't seem to be very stable. Sometimes it doesn't let you save so you have to copy all of your work to a local file, reload the page, and copy your work back. I hope that this gets fixed soon!
- It doesn't have a command-line interface. This means that you can't install npm packages using this method alone.
- You need internet access to work on your Lambdas.

# Method 2 – Cloud9 editor

Amazon recently acquired Cloud9, an online development platform. It runs a very basic version of Ubuntu that is integrated with the rest of the AWS platform.

Search for Cloud9 in the AWS Console, go to the page, and select **Create environment**. From here you give your environment a name and go to the next step.

Here you get to choose what you want to run this environment on. The great thing is that t2.micro is free-tier-eligible, so you can use this method without getting charged anything if you're on the free tier. I've never needed anything more powerful than a t2.micro.

Complete the setup process and you'll end up in your new Cloud9 environment!

The cool thing about this is that you have access to all of your Lambda functions from inside your Cloud9 environment. Click **AWS Resources** and under **Remote Functions**, you'll find all of your functions. Click on the Lambda function you want to edit and then hit the download icon above to import it into your environment:

Accessing remote Lambdas

Once that's done, it'll just be like you're working on it locally.

Once you're finished, just select the function you've been working on from the local list and hit the upload button. Within a few seconds, it'll be live with all your changes.

**The advantages**:

- Again, this is all remote so you don't need to worry about forgetting to commit your work or saving it to a memory stick if you work on multiple machines.
- Accessing your functions and reuploading them is super easy. This is by far the best bit about this method.
- You now have an integrated terminal, allowing you to install npm packages and do everything else you want to do using the terminal.

**The disadvantages**:

- It still has the same stability issues that the Lambda Console editor has. I've had multiple occasions where I've tried to save the function but couldn't, and have had to copy to local, refresh, and recopy to Cloud 9. This becomes very annoying very quickly.
- You need internet access to work on your Lambdas.

# Method 3 – Local editing

I'm going to do this one a little differently. I'll list the advantages and disadvantages of a basic usage and then show you how to make it much better.

**The advantages**:

- Local editing is how most developers will work. We can use our favorite IDE, extensions, and color schemes.
- It's stable (as long as your computer is).
- You can work on your Lambdas without needing an internet connection.

**The disadvantages**:

- There's no fancy button to get and upload your work to AWS
- Your work is local, so having multiple users or just working on multiple devices is more complex

To make this method into the perfect system, we are going to make use of Amazon CLI and Git. It should take about 15 minutes to set up everything we need!

# Creating the best local development environment

As we've already seen, there are some brilliant aspects of writing Lambdas locally, which is why we are going to use it throughout this book. We're going to choose an IDE and install NodeJS and NPM before setting up a folder structure for our Lambdas. Finally, we'll use the AWS CLI and Git to create awesome tools to get rid of the normal disadvantages of working locally.

# Choosing an IDE

Which IDE you use is down to personal preference; there are a few great ones out there, including Atom, Komodo, and Brackets. If you already have a personal favorite then you can use that, but all of the examples will use **Visual Studio Code (VS Code)**.

VS Code is an open source IDE developed by Microsoft and is made for macOS, Linux Windows. It has built-in support for JavaScript, Node, and TypeScript and you can install extensions from the extension library. These extensions are one of the biggest advantages to using VS Code as they allow you to customize so much about your experience. From colored indentations to linting, from better icons to auto-formatters. They vary from the *sort of interesting* to the *making your life far easier*.

As well as the extensions, VS Code has more great features such as an integrated terminal, Git integration, and a built-in debugger. If you've not tried it before, I would recommend trying it out for a week and seeing how it compares to your current IDE of choice.

To install VS Code, just go to `code.visualstudio.com` and download the version you need for your operating system.

# Installing Node and NPM

Node is the runtime that allows us to run JavaScript code on a server. It has gained massive favor over the last few years and is powering applications in almost every sector of technology. It is also one of the runtimes that can be chosen on Lambda functions.

Along with Node, we get **Node Package Manager** (npm), which is the largest ecosystem of open source libraries in the world. This is great for us and we'll be using some of these packages throughout this book.

To install Node and `npm` you can download the installation packages from `nodejs.org` or through a package manager. Make sure that you install at least version 8.11.1 because we will be using *async/await* in our work, and this requires at least version 8. Once you have installed everything you can test that it's working by typing `node -v`; you should get something like `v8.11.1`. You can also test `npm` by typing `npm -v`.

# Folder structure

To properly organize all of your Lambdas it is a good idea to have them all stored in a single folder. This will allow a single script to create and update all of your Lambdas. Within this main folder, having sub-folders containing groups of Lambdas is definitely a good idea. You can very quickly build up a large number of Lambdas.

# Setting up AWS CLI

To upload our work directly to AWS, we can use the AWS CLI. This allows us to manage our AWS services from the command line and create scripts to automate common tasks. For us, the most important CLI commands are the ones that allow us to create and update Lambdas. With automated scripts we now have the ability to quickly and easily create and deploy Lambdas, fixing the first of the *local editing* limitations.

To use the AWS CLI, we first need to set it up. You can install it by typing `npm install -g aws-cli` into your terminal.

Now we need to set up a user for our CLI to log in as. Log in to your AWS Console and navigate to or search for `IAM`. Click **Add user** so we can set up a user for our CLI. You're asked to give the user a name, so choose something like `cli-user` so that it is easily identifiable. Select **Programmatic access**, which will allow us to act as the user remotely, and click **Next: Permissions**.

In the **Permissions** screen, choose to **Attach existing policies directly** and select **AdministratorAccess**. This will let you do whatever you want through your CLI. You can set stricter policies on this user if you want, or if you are giving another person access to your account.

There's another screen before you end up being shown your access keys. Copy your access keys and open a terminal. Run the command `aws configure`, which will ask you for four things:

```
AWS Access Key ID [None]: "Your Access Key ID
"AWS Secret Access Key [None]: "Your Secret Access Key"
Default region name [eu-west-1]:
Default output format [json]:
```

The first two are found on the last page of the user creation. The third must be the region you chose earlier (`eu-west-1` or `us-east-1`), and the last one can be left as default.

# Creating a Lambda using AWS CLI

Now that we've got the CLI set up, we can use it to make our lives much easier. To create a new function, you need to have a folder containing an `index.js` file with a basic Lambda code in. Navigate into that folder in your terminal and now you can run these commands:

```
zip ./index.zip *
aws lambda create-function \
  --function-name your-function-name \
```

```
--runtime nodejs8.10 \
--role your-lambda-role \
 --handler index.handler \
 --zip-file fileb://index.zip
```

Switch out the `your-lambda-role` for the `arn` of the role that you created earlier. You can find this by going back to the `IAM` service in AWS and selecting `Roles` and clicking on your Lambda role:

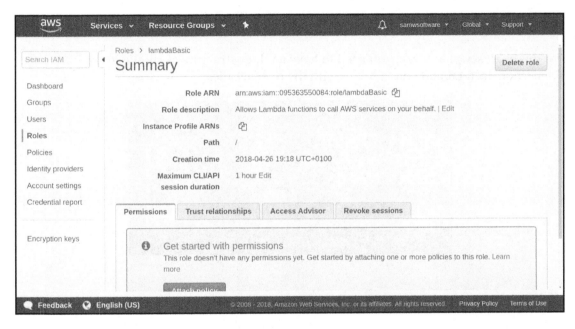

Find your role ARN

When you run this it will return a JSON blob with some information about your newly created Lambda.

If you edit your `index.js` code and want to update the Lambda, then there are three commands you need to run:

```
rm index.zip
zip ./index.zip *
aws lambda update-function-code \
--function-name your-function-name \
--zip-file fileb://index.zip
```

Using these scripts, you can now write your code locally and deploy it to AWS. This is good but it can be improved, which is what we're going to do next.

# AWS CLI build script

These CLI commands are good, but typing this all out every time you want to upload a new Lambda version becomes annoying. We're going to use a build script to automate these commands and add in a few extra features.

 This script is going to be a bash script, so if you are running macOS or Linux then this will work natively. If you are on Windows then you'll need to install a bash terminal on your machine.

For this exact script to work, you need to have a folder structure as shown in the following screenshot. Each Lambda has a folder with the relevant files:

```
▲ 📁 lambdas
    ▲ 📁 example-lambda
        JS index.js
    ▲ 📁 lambda-2
        JS index.js
    ▲ 📁 lambda-3
        JS index.js
```

Folder structure

We will create a script that not only runs the basic AWS CLI commands, but also does extra checks, runs `npm install`, and echos out details about the progress. This script will be executed by running `./build lambda-folder`.

Create a new file called `build.sh` in your `lambdas` folder. Alternatively, you can download this file from `http://bit.ly/chatbot-ch2` and follow along to see how it works.

To start, we will check that exactly one parameter has been passed in the command. `"$#"` means the number of parameters and `-ne 1` means not equal to 1:

```
if [ "$#" -ne 1 ]; then
echo "Usage : ./build.sh lambdaName";
 exit 1;
fi
```

Next, we need to move into the folder for the selected Lambda and check that the folder exists:

```
lambda=${1%/}; // # Removes trailing slashes
echo "Deploying $lambda";
cd $lambda;
if [ $? -eq 0 ]; then
 echo "...."
else
echo "Couldn't cd to directory $lambda. You may have mis-spelled the
lambda/directory name";
exit 1
fi
```

We don't want to upload our Lambda without making sure that we've installed all of the dependencies, so we make sure to run npm install and check that it has been successful:

```
echo "npm installing...";
npm install
if [$? -eq 0 ]; then
    echo "done";
else
    echo "npm install failed";
    exit 1;
fi
```

The last of the setup steps is to check that aws-cli is installed:

```
echo "Checking that aws-cli is installed"
which aws
if [ $? -eq 0 ]; then
 echo "aws-cli is installed, continuing..."
else
echo "You need aws-cli to deploy this lambda. Google 'aws-cli install'"
exit 1
fi
```

With everything set up, we can create our new ZIP file. Before creating the new .zip file, we'll delete the old one. Creating a new one this time is a little bit more advanced than before. We exclude .git, .sh, and .zip files as well as excluding test folders and node_modules/aws-sdk from the file. We can exclude aws-sdk because it is already installed on all Lambda functions and we don't want to upload Git files, bash scripts, or other .zip files:

```
echo "removing old zip"
rm archive.zip;
```

```
echo "creating a new zip file"
zip archive.zip * -r -x .git/\* \*.sh tests/\* node_modules/aws-sdk/\*
\*.zip
```

Now, all there is left to do is to upload it to AWS. We want to make this as easy as possible so we're going to try creating a new function. If that errors then we'll try updating the function. This could be done as a *get* and then *create* or *update*, but a failure to *create* is actually quicker than a *get*:

```
echo "Uploading $lambda to $region";
aws lambda create-function --function-name $lambda --runtime nodejs8.10 --
role arn:aws:iam::095363550084:role/service-role/Dynamo --handler
index.handler --zip-file fileb://index.zip --publish
if [ $? -eq 0 ]; then
  echo "!! Create successful !!"
    exit 1;
fi
aws lambda update-function-code --function-name $lambda --zip-file
fileb://archive.zip --publish
if [ $? -eq 0 ]; then
echo "!! Update successful !!"
else
echo "Upload failed"
echo "If the error was a 400, check that there are no slashes in your
lambda name"
 echo "Lambda name = $lambda"
exit 1;
fi
```

To make the script executable, we need to change the permissions on the file. To do this, we run `chmod +x ./build.sh`.

Now, all you need to do is to navigate to the main folder where the Lambdas function resides and run `./build.sh example-lambda`. If you have Lambdas folders nested in groups, then navigate into the group folders and run `../build.sh lambda-in-group`.

If you want, you can move the build script to your home directory to make execution `~/build.sh lambda-function`, which is only useful if you have Lambdas in separate folders or highly nested folders.

This script could be modified and expanded to include region-specific uploading, batch uploading multiple Lambda functions, Git integration, and lots more.

# Git

A lot of people reading this will use Git already. There's a reason for that—it makes life simpler. Having a Git repository for all of your Lambda functions is a great way to work with teams of developers or by yourself on multiple machines.

Installing Git on your system varies depending on your operating system. Linux users can install Git through the command line, macOS users can install using Homebrew or via download, and Windows users have to install Git via download. Details on exactly how to install for your system are available on `git-scm.com`.

Once you have Git installed, navigate in the terminal to your Lambda folder. When inside that folder, run `git init` to create an empty repository. When you open your Lambda folder in VS Code, you will now have a number hovering over the Git symbol. This means that you have edited that number of files since your last Git commit.

Committing to Git is like taking a snapshot of all of the work in the folder and saving it. This is useful as it allows you to see how your work changes over time. To commit your work (take the snapshot) you have two options.

You can use the Git integration with VS Code to create the commit. Click on the Git symbol with the number hovering over it. When you click on that, it opens the changes menu, showing you all of the files that you have changed since your last commit, or all of your files if this is your first commit. To commit the changed work, type a message into the message box at the top and click the tick above that:

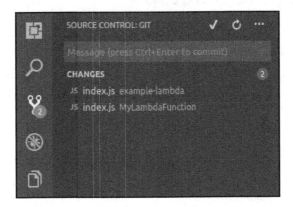

Git commit using VS Code integration

If you want to use the command line you need to enter `git add *` to add all of your changed files to the commit you're about to do. Then type `git commit -m "My first git commit!"`. The text between the quote marks is your commit message.

In both cases, your commit message should describe the changes that you've made in this commit. Your first commit will probably be `"creating my first function"`.

Another massive advantage to Git is that you can easily create remote Git repositories. These are data centers that will store your Git commits so you can access them from anywhere in the world. The major two are GitHub and Bitbucket but there are lots more. They both have free versions, but GitHub is only free for public repositories so anyone can see your work.

Once you've signed up for an account and created a repository, you'll be given a URL for it. In your terminal, navigate to your folder and run `git add remote origin <your url>`. This means that you can send work from your local machine to your online repository. Just type `git push origin master` to send your latest commits to your online repository. Getting them back is just as simple; just type `git pull origin master` and your local code will update to add in any changes made in your repository.

This is great for teams as it allows you to all work on your own machines but be able to get each other's changes.

# Local development setup

To summarize your new local development setup, you have the following:

- A powerful IDE – VS Code
- Amazon CLI-powered build scripts to create and update functions
- Git to store your work remotely and allow easier teamwork

# Summary

In this chapter, we have learned about Amazon Web Services and created an account, giving us access to all of these services.

We created our first Lambda function using the Lambda Console, and advanced it to use multiple functions, template strings, and requiring in code from other files.

Next, we discussed the three main ways to create Lambdas, namely the Lambda Console, Cloud9, and using local development. We also looked at the advantages and disadvantages of each.

Finally, we used the AWS-CLI and Git to make our local development setup far more powerful. The build script that we used allows us to create and update Lambdas without ever having to go onto AWS.

In the next chapter, we will learn to build our first Alexa Skills using the Alexa Skills Kit.

# Questions

1. Name the three main ways to create and edit Lambda functions.
2. What does AWS stand for?
3. What are the two main limitations of a basic local development setup?
4. What tools do we use to improve our local development setup?

# Creating Your First Alexa Skill

# 3

This chapter will introduce you to the process required to build Alexa Skills, and together we will create our first Alexa Skill. We'll learn how to build and test our skill to make sure that everything is working.

We'll then create a second Alexa Skill that has a more realistic conversation with the user. This skill will go through a series of questions to gather a set of information, which we'll use to decide which car is best suited to the user. This will also cover accessing data from remote storage.

The last thing we will cover in this chapter is deploying your skill, allowing you to publish your skills for the world to use.

This chapter will cover the following:

- Creating our first Alexa Skill
- Using Alexa SDK in a Lambda to handle the requests from Alexa
- Testing your Lambda
- Creating a more complex Alexa Skill that uses data stored on S3
- Deploying your Alexa Skill

## Technical requirements

In this chapter, we will be creating a Lambda function for our skill and we'll be creating and deploying it using the local development setup that we created in the previous chapter.

All of the code used in this chapter is available at `http://bit.ly/chatbot-ch3`.

# Alexa Skills Kit

To create our first Alexa Skill, we're going to use Alexa Skills Kit. Search for **Alexa Skills Kit** or go to `www.developer.amazon.com/alexa-skills-kit` and you should see a screen with a **Create Skill** or **Start a Skill** button:

Creating your first skill

Start by giving your skill a name. This should be something that describes what the skill does. For this, we can call it `Hi`. Click **Next** and you'll be able to select a model for your skill. We want to choose **Custom** so we can create the skill exactly how we want:

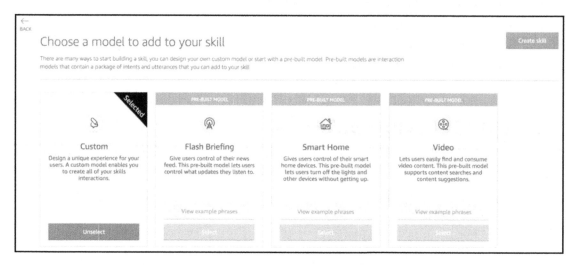

Creating a custom skill

Click **Create skill** and once the setup has finished, you'll end up on the Alexa Skill builder page. To get started, we need to click on **Invocation Name** in the left-hand menu. This is where we set up the command that starts our skill. I'm going to use `sams demo bot` for this first skill. When you create bigger skills, it is a good idea to spend some time thinking about what you use as your invocation phrase and practice saying it out loud:

## Invocation

Users say a skill's invocation name to begin an interaction with a particular custom skill.

For example, if the invocation name is "daily horoscopes", users can say:

**User: Alexa, ask daily horoscopes for the horoscope for Gemini**

## Skill Invocation Name  ⑦

e.g. tide pooler

Skill invocation

Now that we can start our skill, we need to create an intent so that our skill does something. Click the **Add** button, next to the intents in the left-hand menu, to create a new intent. Here, you have the option to **Create custom intent** or to use an existing intent from Amazon's library. Most of Amazon's intents are to do with page navigation or music control, so we're going with a custom intent.

Give your intent a name that describes what the intent is going to do. In our case, it is to say `Hello`, so that is what it can be called. Click **Create custom intent** to start editing the intent.

Now that we're in the intent window for our `Hello` intent, we need to add some utterances. As we talked about in `Chapter 1`, *Understanding Chatbots*, these are phrases the user might say to trigger this intent. For this intent, those utterances might be `hi`, `hello`, or `hey`:

Hello utterances

We have completed our first Alexa intent, so we need to save and build this model. At the top of the intents window is a **Save Model** button and a **Build Model** button, so save it and then build it. Building the model sometimes takes a while, so just wait for that to finish.

# Creating a Lambda to handle the request

To handle the intents inside our new Alexa Skill, we need to create a Lambda function. This will contain all of the logic we need to understand the intent and send a reply to the user.

To create a Lambda, we can use any of the methods described in `Chapter 2`, *Getting Started with AWS and Amazon CLI*, but we're going to be using our local development setup. Navigate to your base Lambda folder and create a new folder called `hello-alexa-skill`. Inside that folder, we need to create a new `index.js` file and open it to create our function.

To start, we need to `require` in the `alexa-sdk`, which makes creating the logic for Alexa a lot easier:

```
const Alexa = require('alexa-sdk');
```

Because we are requiring it, we also need to make sure that we have it installed. In the command-line interface, navigate into your `hello-alexa-skill` folder and run the `npm init` command. This process creates a package information and allows you to install other packages in the folder. You can set the values as you go through the setup or use the defaults by hitting *Enter*. Once you've finished the setup, you'll have a file called `package.json`, which contains the configuration for this folder.

To install a new package and add it to our `package.json` file, we can run the `npm install --save package-name` command. We want to install `ask-sdk`, so we need to run `npm install --save ask-sdk`. When this command runs, you'll see a new folder is created, called `node_modules`, which contains all of the code in the installed npm packages.

## Creating handlers

When our intents are triggered by a user saying one of our utterances, we need to handle that inside our code. To do this, we create an object containing a method for each of our intents. Currently, we only have one `hello` intent, so we only need to create one handler:

```
const helloHandler = {
    canHandle(handlerInput) {
        return handlerInput.requestEnvelope.request.type ===
'IntentRequest' &&
            handlerInput.requestEnvelope.request.intent.name === 'hello';
    },
    handle(handlerInput) {
        const speechText = `Hello from Sam's new intent!`;

        return handlerInput.responseBuilder
            .speak(speechText)
            .getResponse();
    }
};
```

This `hello` handler has two parts: `canHandle` and `handle`. The `canHandle` function decides whether this handler can deal with this request, returning true if it can and false if it can't. This is calculated using the request type and intent name. If both match, then this is the correct handler. `handle` is telling Alexa how to respond. For this intent, all we want Alexa to do is to say *Hello from Sam's new intent!* and then get the user's next message.

Now we need to add our `helloHandler` to our skill.

We can add multiple handlers by passing them as multiple parameters to the `.addRequestHandlers` method:

```
exports.handler = Alexa.SkillBuilders.custom()
    .addRequestHandlers(
        helloHandler)
    .lambda();
```

# Building and configuring the Lambda

Now that the function is completed, we can use the build script that we made in `Chapter 2,` *Getting Started with AWS and Amazon CLI*. Run the `./build.sh hello-alexa-skill` command to create our Lambda and deploy it to AWS.

When the build script finishes, navigate to your Lambda console in AWS and you should now see your newly created function. Click on this new `hello-alexa-skill` Lambda to open up the editor.

To allow this Lambda to be triggered by an Alexa Skill, we need to add **Alexa Skills Kit** as a trigger. This is done by clicking on **Alexa Skills Kit** in the designer under **Add triggers**, creating an Alexa Skills Kit trigger appears in the main designer screenshot:

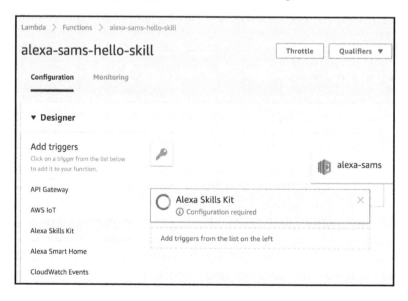

Adding an Alexa Skills Kit trigger

This also opens the **Alexa Skills Kit** configuration section. Here, we need to provide the Alexa App ID for our skill. To find this, open the Alexa Skill Kit console, go to **Endpoint**, and choose Lambda. This will open up a few extra details and options. Our `Skill ID` is the first bit of information and can be copied to our clipboard and inserted into our Lambda configuration:

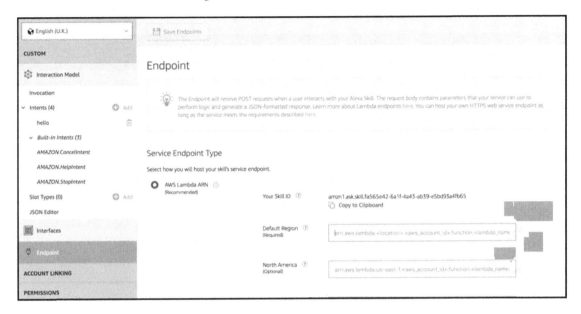

Skill endpoint configuration

Before exiting the Lambda editor, we should find the **ARN** in the upper-right corner of the editor screen. Copy this as we'll need it for the last step in configuring the skill.

# Finishing skill configuration

Now that we have the Lambda configured and the **ARN** in our clipboard, we can go back to our Skill console. Under **Endpoint**, we can insert our Lambda **ARN** into the textbox next to **Default Region**. This makes sure that the skill is triggering the correct Lambda. You can also create different Lambdas for different regions, allowing you to serve specific responses to different groups of people.

Click **Save Endpoints** to save your skill and you have completed your first Alexa Skill. Now comes the fun part: trying out your skill!

# Testing your skills

Now that we've built and deployed our new Alexa Skill, we need to test it out and see whether it works. At the top of the page, there are four tabs: **Build**, **Test**, **Launch**, and **Measure**. We've finished with **Build**, so we can click on **Test**. Click the toggle at the top of the page to enable testing for this skill:

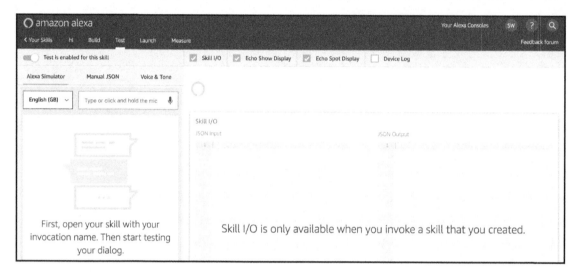

Test screen

To interact with your new skill, you can either type your messages or click and hold the microphone button and talk to your computer like you would with Alexa. To test your skill by talking to it, you will need a microphone on your laptop or PC, and have allowed the web page to access that microphone. As soon as you hit *Enter* or let go of the microphone button, you'll see Alexa loading and then she'll reply with your intent and add the message to the chat window. As well as the response from Alexa, you also get information in the **Skill I/O** section of the screen. If the intent was successfully triggered, you'll get the full **JSON Input** that is sent to your Lambda as well as the response that it has given:

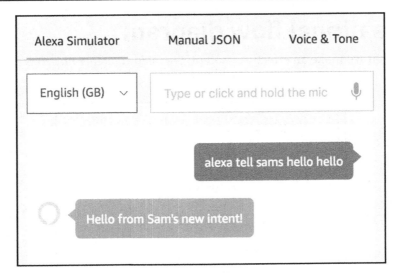

Working hello test

This is what you should get when you chat with your bot. Make sure that you are saying the correct utterances.

## Troubleshooting your skill

Having a few bugs when you first make a skill or Lambda is very normal. The key is to learn how to find the bugs and fix them.

In the *Appendix* of this book is a helpful guide for finding the bugs in Lambdas. Follow those processes and you should have your skill working soon.

## Creating a more useful skill

Creating a skill that says *hello* when you say *hi* is great to see working but it's not very useful. The next skill that we're going to make is going to be a lot more useful.

We're going to create a skill that suggests a model of car to buy, and can provide the user with details about the cars that it suggests.

The data that we will use will contain three sizes of car, two price groups, and an extra category for small cars (number of doors) and for large cars (manual or automatic transmission).

# Conversational flow diagram

To make sure that we make an effective chatbot, we need to create our conversational flow diagram. This starts with our perfect conversation:

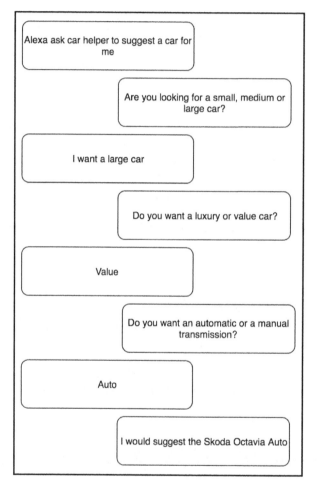

Car conversation

The user chose a large car, therefore, we had to ask them the price group as well as what type of transmission they want. This logic is going to become apparent in the conversation flow diagram. We can create similar conversations for users who choose medium or small cars, where all of the conversations would be slightly different. When there are different questions based on what the user has previously said, you can end up with hundreds of different conversations. This is where conversation flow diagrams really become useful.

In this conversation flow diagram, we have a very important *logic* component. It sees whether the user has chosen a small, medium, or large car, and directs the conversation based on that. This means that we can now show lots of different conversation options in one diagram:

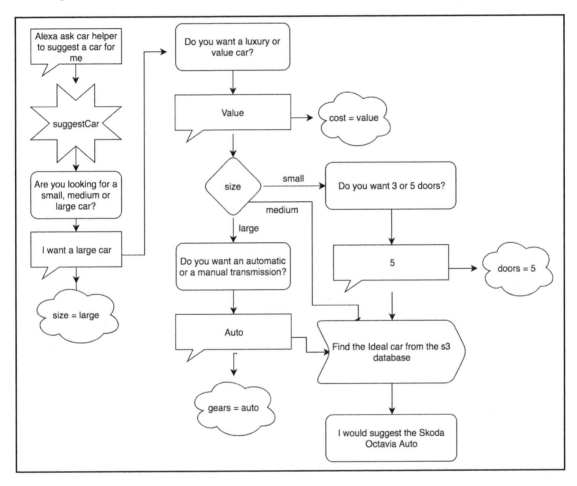

Car flow diagram

Toward the end of the flow, we also have a lookup to find the ideal car for the user. This is something completely new that we'll cover in detail later in this chapter.

# Creating the Alexa Skill

We start making this skill in the same way as before. Go into your Alexa Skills Kit developer console and choose **Create Skill**. Choose a suitable name, such as `carHelper`, and select a **Custom** skill.

Now that we're in the skill console again, we need to start at the top by setting the invocation utterance. Enter `Car Helper` or something similar that is memorable and easy to say.

# Creating an Intent

Now we can move on to the main part of the skill—adding the intent. For this, we add a new intent and we can call it `whichCar`, as we are trying to help the user choose *which car* to get.

The first thing this intent needs is utterances. Add in phrases that the user might say if they are wanting to find out which car to buy:

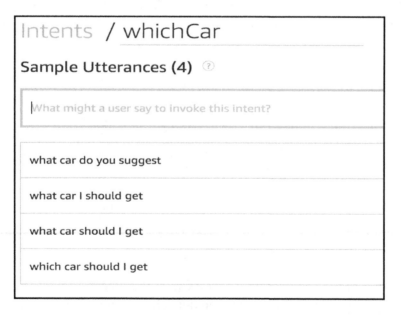

Intent utterances

# Internal Slots

This is where we need to start making the skill more advanced than last time. We need to store information such as the size, cost, doors, and whether the user wants to have automatic or manual gears. To add a new slot, scroll down to **Intent Slots** and click on **Create a new slot**. In here, you can name your slot and then add that to your intent by pressing *Enter* or clicking the **+** icon. Do this for **size**, **cost**, **doors**, and **gears**:

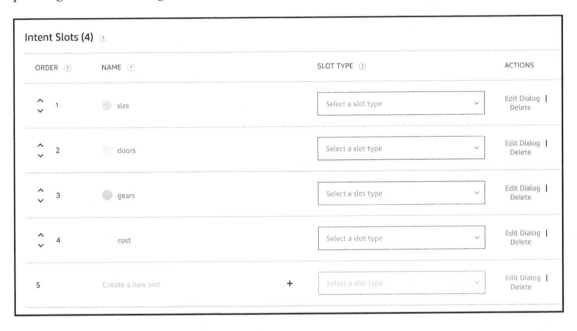

Intent Slots

Before we can store any information in these slots, we need to set their **SLOT TYPE**. The number of doors is simple as it is just a number, so **AMAZON.NUMBER** can be chosen as its slot type. For the other three slots, it's a bit more complicated.

We need to create custom slot types for these three slots. To create a new slot type, click the **+** next to **Slot Types**, which will take you to the **Add Slot Type** screen. Enter the name for your new slot type and click **Create custom slot type**. We will start with a slot type called `carSize`.

Now you are in the slot type editing screen, and you'll see your new slot type in the menu on the left. We need to add the three values that the user can select: large, medium, and small. This would work as it is, but what if a user says big instead of large? We can capture these too using synonyms. We can enter as many new values as we want, and if a user says them, it will be registered as the main value:

Car size slot type

This process needs to be repeated to create a carCost slot type with values of luxury and value, and a carGear slot type with values of automatic and manual. You should also add synonyms for each of these values to improve the flexibility of your bot.

Now that we have created the three new slot types, we can add them to our slots. You should now find your new slot types in the slot type drop-down menu. Make sure each of the slots has the correct slot type, and we're almost finished with the skill editor.

We know that the user is always going to be asked for their choice in size and cost, so we can set these two slots to be required. Clicking on the slot name under the intent will take you to the slot config screen where we have the **Slot Type**, **Slot Filling**, and **Slot Confirmation** sections.

In the **Slot Filling** section, there is a toggle to change the slot to being required. When we click that toggle, it opens more settings for us to configure. The first is the **Alexa speech prompts** where we can type a prompt that will get the user to fill in the slot correctly:

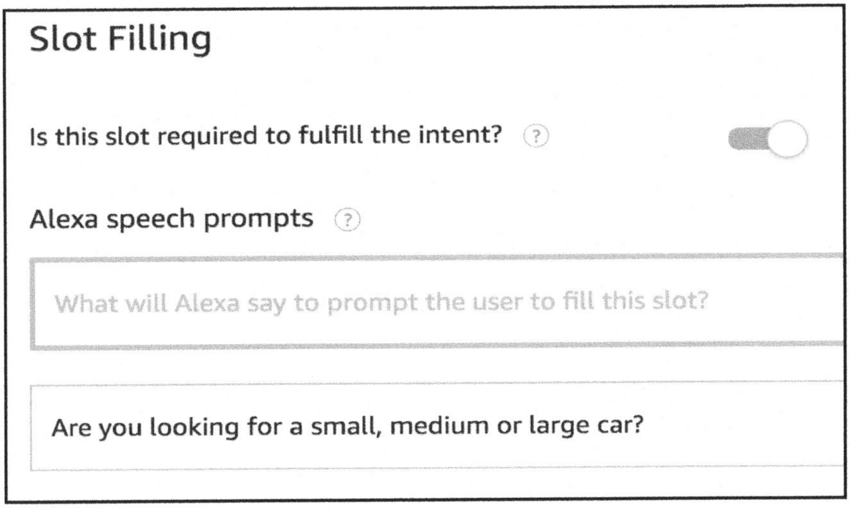

## Slot Filling

**Is this slot required to fulfill the intent?** ⑦

**Alexa speech prompts** ⑦

What will Alexa say to prompt the user to fill this slot?

Are you looking for a small, medium or large car?

Required slot

We can also enter utterances that the user might reply with. The first one can simply be the size, so we need to type the slot name wrapped in curly braces. As well as just saying `large`, the user might say `I want a large car` or `I'm looking for a medium car`. To deal with these, we type those utterances but change large and medium for **{size}**:

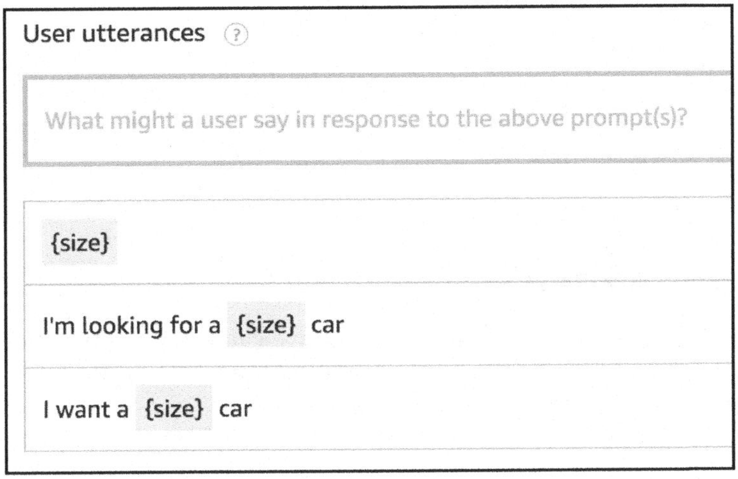

**User utterances** ⑦

What might a user say in response to the above prompt(s)?

{size}

I'm looking for a {size} car

I want a {size} car

Slot utterances

Do the same process for *cost*, using utterances such as I want a {cost} car. Add a few other utterances if you want to.

We don't need to do this for gears or doors as they aren't required in every conversation, but we'll be able to ask for them from our Lambda.

Once you have created the three custom slots and added the slot types to all of your slots, you should have intent slots that look like this:

Slot types completed

# Finding the Skill ID

The last thing to do is find and copy the Skill ID so we can use it in our Lambda. Select **Endpoint** in the left-hand menu and choose **AWS Lambda ARN** as the service endpoint method. This will expose the Skill ID that we need to copy.

# Creating the Lambda

Now that we have done the console setup, we can build the Lambda that will handle the logic behind the skill.

Start by creating a new folder in your `lambdas` folder, naming it something appropriate, such as `carHelper`. Inside, we need to create an `index.js` file and run `npm init`. We are using `alexa-sdk` again so we need to run `npm install --save alexa-sdk`.

With the setup ready, we can start writing the Lambda. We can start with a Lambda that looks very similar to the Lambda we created in our first function:

```
const Alexa = require('alexa-sdk');

exports.handler = Alexa.SkillBuilders.custom()
    .addRequestHandlers()
    .lambda();
```

The first handler we are going to create is to handle a launch request. This is when a user says something like `"Alexa start car helper"`; our skill is launched but no intent is triggered. We need to help them trigger one of our intents by telling them what to say to trigger our intent. We can then add this as our first handler in `.addRequestHandlers()`:

```
const LaunchRequestHandler = {
    canHandle(handlerInput) {
        return handlerInput.requestEnvelope.request.type ===
'LaunchRequest';
    },
    handle(handlerInput) {
        const speechText = `Hi there, I'm Car Helper. You can ask me to
suggest a car for you.`;

        return handlerInput.responseBuilder
            .speak(speechText)
            .reprompt(speechText)
            .getResponse();
    }
};
```

# Handling the whichCar Intent

We can start dealing with our `whichCar` intent. We start by creating the `WhichCarHandler` and adding it to the list in `addRequestHandlers()`:

```
const WhichCarHandler = {
    canHandle(handlerInput) {
        return handlerInput.requestEnvelope.request.type ===
'IntentRequest' &&
            handlerInput.requestEnvelope.request.intent.name ===
'whichCar';
    },
    async handle(handlerInput) {}
}
```

Inside this `handler` function, the first thing that we need to do is to get the slots from the event. We can use `es6` destructuring to simplify our code:

```
const slots = handlerInput.requestEnvelope.request.intent.slots;
const {size, cost, gears, doors} = slots;
```

We now have access to all four of our slot variables. Even though we created our slot types, we need to check that we have valid values. We'll start with size and cost as we know that we always need values for those slots:

```
if (!size.value || !(size.value === 'large' || size.value === 'medium' ||
size.value === 'small')) {
    const slotToElicit = 'size';
    const speechOutput = 'What size car do you want? Please say either
small, medium or large.';
    return handlerInput.responseBuilder
        .speak(speechOutput)
        .addElicitSlotDirective(slotToElicit)
        .getResponse();
}

if (!cost.value || !(cost.value === 'luxury' || cost.value === 'value')){
    console.log('incorrect cost')
    const slotToElicit = 'cost';
    const speechOutput = 'Are you looking for a luxury or value car?';
    return handlerInput.responseBuilder
        .speak(speechOutput)
        .addElicitSlotDirective(slotToElicit)
        .getResponse();
}
```

These two blocks of code check that the slots exist and then check that they equal one of the expected responses. If the slot isn't filled or doesn't equal one of the expected values, we get Alexa to ask for the slot again using .addElicitSlotDirective.

If the request has got past these two blocks, we know that we have a valid size and cost. In our flow diagram, this is where we had a logic step to decide which path to send them down, so that is what we need to implement now.

If the user chose a large car, we need to see whether they have chosen a gear yet. If they haven't, we ask them whether they want to have an automatic or manual transmission. We do the same process for small cars and the number of doors:

```
if (size.value === 'large' && ( !gears.value || !(gears.value ===
'automatic' || gears.value === 'manual') )){
    // missing or incorrect gears
    const slotToElicit = 'gears';
    const speechOutput = 'Do you want an automatic or a manual
transmission?';
    return handlerInput.responseBuilder
        .speak(speechOutput)
        .addElicitSlotDirective(slotToElicit)
        .getResponse();
}

if (size.value === 'small' && ( !doors.value || !(doors.value == 3 ||
doors.value == 5) )){
    // missing or incorrect doors
    const slotToElicit = 'doors';
    const speechOutput = 'Do you want 3 or 5 doors?';
    return handlerInput.responseBuilder
        .speak(speechOutput)
        .addElicitSlotDirective(slotToElicit)
        .getResponse();
}
```

If the request has got past this point, there are three possibilities:

- They chose a small car and have selected the number of doors
- They chose a medium car so didn't need to choose doors or gears
- They chose a large car and have chosen their gears

The next step is to find the best car based on the user choices. To choose the best car, we need to have a selection of cars to sort from. We can create an object outside of the handler to store the data we need to sort the cars:

```
const cars = [
    {name: 'fiat500', size:'small', cost: 'luxury', doors: 3, gears:
'manual'},
    {name: 'fordFiesta', size:'small', cost: 'luxury', doors: 5, gears:
'manual'},
    {name: 'hyundaiI10', size:'small', cost: 'value', doors: 3, gears:
'manual'},
    {name: 'peugeot208', size:'small', cost: 'value', doors: 5, gears:
'manual'},
    {name: 'vauxhallAstra', size:'medium', cost: 'value', doors: 5, gears:
'manual'},
    {name: 'vwGolf', size:'medium', cost: 'luxury', doors: 5, gears:
'manual'},
    {name: 'scodaOctaviaAuto', size:'large', cost: 'value', doors: 5,
gears: 'automatic'},
    {name: 'fordCmax', size:'large', cost: 'value', doors: 5, gears:
'manual'},
    {name: 'mercedesEClass', size:'large', cost: 'luxury', doors: 5,
gears: 'automatic'},
    {name: 'vauxhallInsignia', size:'large', cost: 'luxury', doors: 5,
gears: 'manual'}
];
```

With this object containing all of the car options we want, we need to find the car that is best for the user. To do this, we can use the `Array.filter()` function. This function goes through each item in an array and applies a function to it. If the function returns true, the item is kept in the array, otherwise, it is removed:

```
// find the ideal car
let chosenCar = cars.filter(car => {
    return (car.size === size.value && car.cost === cost.value &&
        (gears.value ? car.gears === gears.value : true) &&
        (doors.value ? car.doors == doors.value: true));
});
```

To find the best car for the user, this filter function checks that `car.size` and `car.cost` equal what the user selected, and then uses ternary expressions to check the gears and doors. If the user has selected a gear type or a number of doors, it checks whether the car information matches the user's choice, otherwise it returns `true`.

When we run this function, we get back the car that matches the user's choices. If the user has chosen a small, luxury car with 3 doors, then the chosenCar will equal [{name: 'fiat500', size:'small', cost: 'luxury', doors: 3, gears: 'manual'}].

Before we get more details on the chosen car, we need to check that our function chose a car. This can be done by checking that our new chosenCar array has a length of 1. If it doesn't, there has been some sort of error and we need to let the user know. Add this code after our filter method:

```
if (chosenCar.length !== 1) {
    const speechOutput = `Unfortunately I couldn't find the best car for
you. You can say "suggest a car" if you want to try again.`;
    return handlerInput.responseBuilder
        .speak(speechOutput)
        .getResponse();
}
```

# Amazon S3

Now that we have the chosen car, we can get some more information on that car from an S3 bucket. S3 buckets allow us to store objects and access them from wherever we want.

To create an S3 bucket, search for S3 in the AWS console. On the S3 page, click the **Create bucket** button to start the creation process. Choose a name for your bucket, noting that the name has to be unique across all buckets on S3. Adding your name or an alias onto the start or end of the bucket name can help make your bucket unique. For this example, we don't need to set up any other properties or permissions on the bucket, so we can just click on **Next** until we get to the end.

With your new bucket created, we can start to create data that will be uploaded into it. Uploading data to an S3 bucket is really easy; click on the bucket that you want to upload into and click the **Upload** button. You can then either drag and drop your files in or click **Add files** to upload your files in a more traditional way. For this project, we don't need to set any of the permissions or properties for these files.

All of the data that we're going to upload is available at http://bit.ly/chatbot-ch3 in the car-data folder. We'll have a look at one example file to see what data we are going to access:

```
{
    "make": "Vauxhall",
    "model": "Astra",
    "rrp": 16200,
```

```
    "fuelEcon": "44-79 mpg",
    "dimensions": "4.258 m L x 1.799 m W x 2.006 m H",
    "NCAPSafetyRating": "5 star",
    "cargo": 370
}
```

With this information, we can give the user a good summary of the car that our chatbot has suggested for them. This could be expanded, but providing too much data to the user may make the interaction too complicated.

# Accessing our S3 data

Now that we have all of our data in our S3 bucket and have chosen a car based on the user's choices, we need to get the relevant data. To do this, we can use `aws-sdk` to interact with S3 from our Lambda.

At the top of our Lambda, we need to require in *AWS* so that we can use the *S3* method. Add these two lines to the top of this Lambda:

```
const AWS = require('aws-sdk');
var s3 = new AWS.S3();
```

Now that we have access to the S3 methods on AWS, we can get the JSON for our chosen car. At the end of our `whichCar` handler, add the following code:

```
var params = {
    Bucket: YOUR BUCKET NAME,
    Key: `${chosenCar[0].name}.json`
};

return new Promise((resolve, reject) => {
    s3.getObject(params, function(err, data) {
        if (err) { // an error occurred
            console.log(err, err.stack);
            reject(handleS3Error(handlerInput));
        } else { // successful response
            console.log(data);
            resolve(handleS3Data(handlerInput, data));
        }
    });
})
```

The first part of this code snippet is choosing where and what data we are trying to access. Make sure that you put in your bucket name. The key is generated using a template string so that we get the file related to the car we chose for the user.

We then return a promise that contains the `s3.getObject()` method, passing in our `params` and a `callback` function. The callback from the `.getObject()` method passes the `err` and `data` parameters. If there is an error, we will `reject` a function called `handleS3Error`. If it succeeds, we'll `resolve` the `handleS3Data` function. We'll create these functions later.

# Adding S3 permissions

Because we are now accessing data from S3, we also need to update the **Execution role** to include S3 read-only. In your AWS console, navigate to **IAM** which is where you control your users, roles, and policies.

In the menu on the left, select **Roles** and you should see a list of your roles. If this is your first time using AWS, you'll only have one role: **LambdaBasic**. When you select it, you are taken to a summary page where there is an **Attach policy** button. We need to attach *S3* permissions so we can click that button.

This opens up a list of all of the policies that are available on your account. Amazon has made hundreds of default policies for almost every scenario. We're going to search for `S3`. We should get at least four options, which include *Redshift*, *FullAccess*, *ReadOnly*, and *QuickSight*. As we're only going to be getting data from S3, we can tick the **AmazonS3ReadOnlyAccess** tickbox and then the **Attach policy** button in the lower-right corner:

Adding Amazon S3 permissions

# Dealing with our data

Having done the request to S3, we have received our data or an error. Either way, we need to deal with it and send a response to the user. We'll create two new functions that deal with either the data or an error:

```
const handleS3Error = handlerInput => {
    const speechOutput = `I've had a problem finding the perfect car for
you.`
    return handlerInput.responseBuilder
        .speak(speechOutput)
        .getResponse();
};

function handleS3Data(data){
    let body = JSON.parse(data.Body);
    console.log('body= ', body);
    let { make, model, rrp, fuelEcon, dimensions, NCAPSafetyRating, cargo}
= body;
    let speech = `I think that a ${make} ${model} would be a good car for
you.
    They're available from ${rrp} pounds, get ${fuelEcon} and have a
${cargo} litre boot.`;
    return handlerInput.responseBuilder
        .speak(speechOutput)
        .getResponse();
}
```

The error function tells the user that we couldn't find the best car for them, while the data function creates a short description of the car using the data. We need to parse the body of the data because the data comes down as a buffer. We need to convert the buffer to a format that we can use.

# Testing our Lambda

With the last skill, the Lambda was simple enough that we could get away with not testing it. This Lambda is more complicated, with multiple places where we could have an error, so we're going test it properly.

In the Lambda console, find your function and open it up. Once inside, click on the dropdown next to **Test** and choose **Configure test events**. Make sure that the **Create new test event** option is selected and we can use a template of **Alexa Intent - GetNewFact**.

Most of the template can be left as default, but we need to change the slots and `intentName` (lines 20 and 21) as well as the application IDs (lines 10 and 35). Start by changing `intentName` to equal the intent that we created (`whichCar`). Next, we can add the slots that we have available. For now, we can set all of them to *null* as that is what they will be when they haven't been populated yet:

```
"slots": {
    "size": null,
    "cost": null,
    "gears": null,
    "doors": null
},
"name": "whichCar"
```

Using the ARN that you got from the Alexa Skill console **Endpoint** section, change the value for `applicationId` at line 10 and 40.

Call this intent `whichCarEmpty` and click **Create**.

Before we run this test, we can think about what we expect to happen. Because there are no slots filled, we expect that it will fail at the `size` check, therefore we will get a response asking us what size of car we want. It is always good to work out what you expect to happen before running a test. It helps you build your code understanding, and if you don't get that response, it raises a red flag in your mind.

Now we can click **Test** and we should get **Execution result: succeeded** and a response with an output speech of "**What size car do you want? Please say either small, medium or large**".

This is what we expected so that is great! If you didn't get this response, look at the error message and use that to figure out what may have gone wrong. There is a helpful section in the *Appendix* that can be used to debug common Lambda errors.

With this test working, we can create another test that has some filled slots. Click the testing dropdown and select **Configure test events** again. Make sure that **Create new test event** is selected, but this time choose **whichCarEmpty** as the template. This means that we know the application IDs are correct and the only things we need to change are the slots. Change the slots to the following code:

```
"slots": {
    "size": { "value": "large"},
    "cost": { "value": "luxury"},
    "gears": { "value": "automatic"},
    "doors": { "value": null}
},
```

Save this test as **whichCarLargeLuxuryAuto**. When you run this test, you should get a successful response of the following:

**"I think that a Mercedes-Benz would be a good car for you. They're available from 35,150 pounds, get 32-66 mpg and have a 425 litre boot."**

You can create tests for each of the possible combinations of results, but since we know that our Lambda is responding and is accessing S3, we know that all of the code is working.

# Finishing the Alexa Skills Kit Configuration

To finish the configuration of our skill, we need to get the ARN of our Lambda. Copy that from the top of the Lambda page or from the result of your build script and go to the Alexa Skills Kit console. Paste it into **Default Region** and save the endpoint. That is all we need to do before we can start testing our skill.

# Testing

Now we can try out our new skill. Here you can see a conversation that I had with my car helper bot:

Testing the car helper skill

This skill isn't perfect – it doesn't respond to every utterance that you might say and there is a lot more the skill could do. The good thing is you now know everything you need to fix all of those issues.

# Launching your skill

To launch your skill to the Alexa Skill Store, we need to move to the next tab. This is where you will set up the information that will be present on the Alexa Skill Store. You need to give your skill a unique name, short and long descriptions, and example utterances. Then you get to upload an icon and select the category and keywords for your skill. The category and keywords should be carefully considered as this is probably how users are going to find your skills.

The last part on this page is the *privacy policy* and *terms of use* URLs. You need to have these if you are going to have a skill in the skills store. There are lots of examples out there and they shouldn't be very complicated for skills that don't store or even ask for user information. Any app that does use and store user information will need a more detailed privacy policy and it may be worth contacting a lawyer:

Launch setup

The next page asks you a number of privacy and compliance questions about your skill. Answer these honestly and then provide some information to the person who will be testing your skill before it gets deployed.

Next, we have to choose the availability of our skill. We can use this to only allow certain organizations to access the skill. This can be useful if you've created a specialized skill for a company and don't want other people using it. You can also select the countries where the skill will be available. You could limit it to one or two countries or let everyone use it.

The last page is a review page where it tells you whether there is anything that your submission is missing. When you fix everything, you can click **Submit for review**. While the skill is in testing, you won't be able to edit the configuration of the skill. You can still edit your Lambdas, but doing so can cause your skill to be rejected.

Once it's been tested and approved, you'll have a live Alexa Skill!

# Summary

This chapter showed us how to do a lot of new things. We started by creating our first Alexa Skill using Alexa Skills Kit. This involved learning about and creating intents, slots, and utterances. With the configuration completed, we created a Lambda to handle the request using Alexa-SDK. This Lambda is where we defined the response that would be sent to the user. Finally, we built and tested our new Alexa Skill using the built-in testing tools.

Having made a basic first skill, we started to create a more useful second skill. We used a custom slot type and applied it to slots in our intents. We then used Amazon's S3 service to store the data we needed before using AWS SDK to easily get the data and use it in our Lambda.

Using the skills learned in this chapter, you can go build a huge range of powerful skills for Alexa.

In the next chapter we'll learn to access APIs, allowing us to create much more powerful skills.

# Questions

1. What is the tool we use in Lambdas for dealing with Alexa requests?
2. What three things do we need to do to connect a Lambda to an Alexa Skill?
3. What is the method we use to get information from our S3 bucket?

4. What do we have to do to the body response from S3 and why?
5. How do we create a Lambda test?

# Further reading

If you want to try out different types of response, have a look through the Alexa SDK response builder docs: `https://ask-sdk-for-nodejs.readthedocs.io/en/latest/Building-Response.html`.

We have only used S3 to get data that we manually stored; there are other methods that allow more S3 functionality: `https://docs.aws.amazon.com/AWSJavaScriptSDK/latest/AWS/S3.html`.

# 4
# Connecting Your Alexa Skills to External APIs

In this chapter, we will expand upon the basics we learned from the previous chapter, to improve the functionality and user experience of Alexa. We'll increase the functionality by learning to use external APIs to interact with services provided by other people. Then, we'll increase the user experience by giving our chatbot some memory of the existing conversation and also using a **speech synthesis markup language (SSML)** to control the way that Alexa talks to the user.

To enable us to learn this, we're going to build a weather skill for Alexa. You will be able to ask for the current or five-day forecast for 200,000 cities across the world.

The following topics will be covered in this chapter:

- Accessing and interacting with an external API
- Storing session memory using session attributes
- Using SSML to control the way that Alexa talks with the user

## Technical requirements

In this chapter, we will be creating a Lambda function for our skill, and we will deploy it using the local development setup that we discussed in Chapter 2, *Getting Started with AWS and Amazon CLI*.

We'll be using the **Open Weather Map API** to get weather data based on the user requests. We will go through the process of creating an account and getting an API key.

We'll use Postman to test the requests that we are going to make to the Open Weather Map API. It is a cross-platform app that can be installed at `getpostman.com`.

All of the code required for this chapter can be found at `http://bit.ly/chatbot-ch4`.

# External APIs

An **Application Programming Interface (API)** is an interface that you can send requests to, and it will give you a response. These are used to let other people control parts of your software, whether that is getting information from the API database, changing a user's settings, or getting the API to send a text.

They are a very powerful tool for developers, giving you access to more data and services than you could ever gather or build on your own.

External APIs don't have to be built by someone else. If you have a system that you want to access from the chatbot, you can add API access, or you might already have an API built for it. Using an API to separate sections of your code or company can be a good way to allow and improve modularization.

# Open Weather Map API

The Open Weather Map API is a very powerful API that lets you get the current weather as well as the weather forecast for 200,000 cities around the world. The best part is that there is a free tier that allows you to make 60 requests a minute about current weather and five-day forecasts. This allows us to develop an Alexa Skill that uses real-world data without subscribing to a monthly fee.

To access this API, we need to create an account to get an API key. Go to `OpenWeatherMap.org` and go to **Sign Up** in the upper-right corner of the page. Enter your details, read the terms and conditions, and sign up. You'll then be prompted to give the reason that you are using the API. There's no *Alexa* option, so you can choose **Mobile apps development,** as that is the closest to our real usage.

Now that you're logged in, you can access your API key. This is used on any request you make to the API so that it can check that you have the right permissions for making the request. Navigate to **API keys,** and find the **Default** key for your account. We'll be using that key throughout this project to make sure that you can find it again:

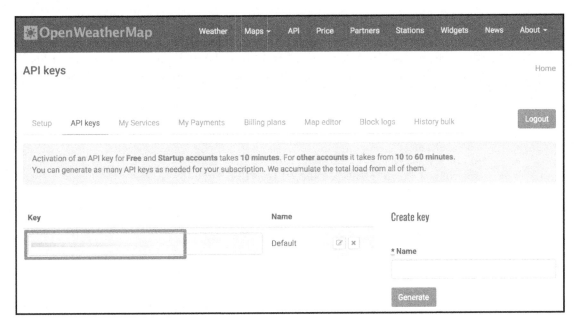

OpenWeatherMap API key

With our API key, we can now look at the requests we can make. On the **API** page, there is a list of different APIs, but the ones that we have access to are **Current weather data** and **5 day / 3-hour forecast**. Underneath each of these sections is a button to go to the **API doc,** and we're going to look at the API docs for **Current weather data**.

There are three ways to request the data on the **Current weather data** API: **Call current weather data for one location**, **Call current weather data for several cities**, and **Bulk downloading**. We're only going to be getting data for one location at a time.

Within the **Call current weather data for one location** section, there are also a few different ways to select the area. You can provide the city name, city ID, geographic coordinates, or the ZIP code. The user is going to be telling us a city name, so it makes the most sense to use that data.

There are two ways to get the current weather data for a city by name:

```
https://api.openweathermap.org/data/2.5/weather?q={city name}
https://api.openweathermap.org/data/2.5/weather?q={city name},{country
code}
```

Whenever we call either of these endpoints, we will get a response in a predefined format. It is good to know how the data will be returned so we can deal with it properly inside our skill. The **Weather parameters in API respond** section of the web page gives us examples of responses, as well as a list of the features, with a short description of each. This is an example of the response that can come back from a request:

```
{
    "city": {
        "id":1851632,
        "name":"Shuzenji",
        "coord": { "lon":138.933334, "lat":34.966671 },
        "country": "JP",
        "cod":"200",
        "message":0.0045,
        "cnt":38,
        "list":[{
            "dt":1406106000,
            "main":{
                "temp":298.77,
                "temp_min":298.77,
                "temp_max":298.774,
                "pressure":1005.93,
                "sea_level":1018.18,
                "grnd_level":1005.93,
                "humidity":87,
                "temp_kf":0.26},
            "weather":[{"id":804,"main":"Clouds","description":"overcast
clouds","icon":"04d"}],
            "clouds":{"all":88},
            "wind":{"speed":5.71,"deg":229.501},
            "sys":{"pod":"d"},
            "dt_txt":"2014-07-23 09:00:00"
        }]
    }
}
```

# Creating our weather skill

Creating the weather skill is going to follow the same steps as the previous skills that we have created. This is a great process to follow whenever you are creating any new Alexa skill. To recap the process, it is as follows:

- Create a conversational flow from perfect conversations
- Create the skill on Alexa Skills Kit, including all intents, slots, and utterances
- Create the Lambda to handle the requests
- Test the skill
- Improve the skill

# Conversation flow design

Most of the conversations that the users will have with this skill are quite simple. There are only really two things that the user can ask about: the location and the data for the forecast. Here is an example of a perfect conversation:

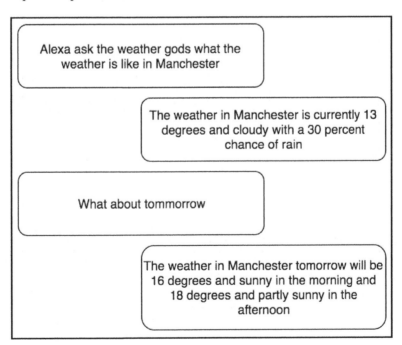

Weather conversation

The interesting thing about this conversation is that both the questions are similar. What is the weather in {location} {date}?

This means that we can handle them both with a single intent. That intent needs to check whether they have given a location and a date and then use those two things to call the API. The flow diagram for this intent will look as follows:

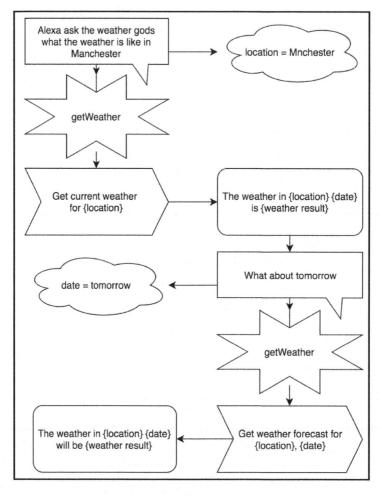

Weather flow diagram

The difference between this flow and the flows that we've worked with before is that the user can go through one intent multiple times in one conversation, usually with different slot values. We could build separate intents for `current weather`, `weather change Date`, and `weather change location`, but they would all do similar things.

# Creating the skill on Alexa Skills Kit

We need to get started using the Alexa Skills Kit developer console. Click the **Create Skill** button, name your skill, and select **Custom** as the skill type.

The first thing that we do whenever we create a new skill adds an invocation phrase.

 Doing it as soon as you create the skill means that you don't forget to fill it in later. You can change the phrase at any point before you publish your skill.

Next, we need to create our `getWeather` intent. Add a new custom intent called `getWeather` and then we can start filling the intent out.

Users are going to trigger this intent with lots of different utterances. We're also going to learn how to populate slots from the user utterance. Start by adding our two slots to the intent, `location` and `date`. The slot type for location can be **AMAZON.US_CITY**, and data can be **AMAZON.DATE**. You can select `GB_CITY`, `AT_CITY`, `DE_CITY`, or `EUROPE_CITY` if you want a better city recognition for your area:

| Intent Slots (2) ⓘ | | | |
|---|---|---|---|
| ORDER ⓘ | NAME ⓘ | SLOT TYPE ⓘ | ACTIONS |
| ⌃ 1 ⌄ | location | AMAZON.US_CITY ⌄ | Edit Dialog \| Delete |
| ⌃ 2 ⌄ | date | AMAZON.DATE ⌄ | Edit Dialog \| Delete |
| 3 | Create a new slot ＋ | Select a slot type ⌄ | Edit Dialog \| Delete |

Intent slots

With the slots created, we can create our utterances. These utterances will be different than our normal utterances, as we need to fill the slots at the same time. This can be demonstrated with an utterance such as what is the weather like in London. The slot that we are trying to fill is a location with the value of London. To capture this slot, we can use a curly brace method where the intent becomes what is the weather like in {location}. This means that whatever value is typed instead of {location} will be captured and stored in the **location** slot.

This can be done for other similar utterances. What about tomorrow becomes what about {date} and an utterance of what is the weather like tomorrow in New York becomes what is the weather like {date} in {location}. This capture of slots from the initial utterance is very powerful, as it means that we don't have to ask the user for the value of each slot. Asking a series of questions like that results in a very unnatural conversation. Here are a few examples of sample utterances:

---

## Sample Utterances (6) ⓘ

What might a user say to invoke this intent?

---

whats {date} weather in {location}

---

what about for {location}

---

what is the weather like {date}

---

what about {date}

---

what is the weather forecast for {location} {date}

---

Get weather utterances

With the intent slots and utterances completed, we can get the skill ID from the **Endpoint** section before moving on to creating the Lambda to handle the requests.

# Building Lambda to handle the requests

To create our Lambda, we can create a new folder within our `Lambdas` folder and call it `weatherGods`. Inside that folder, we can create an `index.js` file in which we will create our handler. To start, copy the text from the `boilerplate Lambda` folder in this chapter's code repository. We also need to run `npm init` so that we can install `npm` packages later on.

Before starting on the main code, we need to modify our `LaunchRequestHandler`. This can be done by changing the `speechText` variable. For this skill, we can enter a response message of `"You may ask the weather gods about the weather in your city or for a weather forecast"`. This prompts the user to say a phrase that will trigger the `getWeather` intent.

Now we can start on the logic to get the user the weather information that they want. We need to create another handler that will deal with the `getWeather` requests:

```
const GetWeatherHandler = {
    canHandle(handlerInput) {
        return handlerInput.requestEnvelope.request.type ===
'IntentRequest' &&
            handlerInput.requestEnvelope.request.intent.name ===
'getWeather';
    },
    handle(handlerInput) {}
}
```

Before we can get the weather, we need to check that we have values for the location and the date. If we don't have values for either of these, we need to get them:

```
const { slots } = this.event.request.intent;
let { location, date } = slots;
location = location.value || null;
date = date.value || null;

if (!location) {
    let slotToElicit = 'location';
    let speechOutput = 'Where do you desire to know the weather';
    return handlerInput.responseBuilder
        .speak(speechOutput)
        .addElicitSlotDirective(slotToElicit)
```

```
        .getResponse();
}
if (!date){
    date = Date.now()
}
```

You will probably notice that the missing location and date are handled differently. If the location is missing, then we ask the user for the location. If we are missing the date, we set the date to `Date.now()`. This is a design choice because it feels more natural to say `"What's the weather like in LA?"` than `"What's the weather like in LA now?"`. It is often the smaller details such as this that make talking with a good chatbot so much better.

We know that we have a location and a date so can proceed with the rest of the logic. With the location and the date, we can make the request to the Open Weather Maps API.

# Making an API request

Making a request to an API consists of using a `GET`, `PUT`, `POST`, or `DELETE` method on a URL with some optional data. A well-designed API will be designed to have most of the information about the request in the URL. This means that we will be changing the URL based on the user choices.

For the Open Weather Maps API, the URLs that we need to send our requests to are structured as follows:

- **For current weather:** `https://api.openweathermap.org/data/2.5/weather?q={$city},us`
- **For a five-day forecast:** `https://api.openweathermap.org/data/2.5/forecast?q=${city},us`

Unfortunately, the API needs us to define a country code. In this example, we should use *US*, as we selected **US_CITY** as our slot type. If you chose a different slot type, make sure to enter the `ISO 3166` code for your country.

To make a request to these URLs, we need to use a request library. There is an `HTTP` standard library built into a node that can make requests, but there are some other libraries that make our life much simpler. The one we will be using is called `axios`. There are two main reasons to use `axios` over the standard `HTTP` library:

- It is more user-friendly
- It is *promise-based*, so you control the flow of the data

To make a request using `axios`, we first need to install it and require it in. Navigate to your `weatherGods` Lambda folder and run `npm install --save axios` and add `const axios = require('axios');` to the top of the `index.js` file.

Making a request can now be as simple as adding this line of code wherever we want to make the request:

```
axios.get(*URL*)
```

For our requests, we will also need to pass in our API key. For the Open Weather Maps API, we need to add a query string of `appid=${process.env.API_KEY}` at the end of our URL.

We store our API key in environment variables so that it never gets committed to source control (GIT), where it could be accessed by someone else. They can be accessed and changed in your Lambda console. To store an environment variable, scroll down in your Lambda console to **Environment variables** and enter the key and value you want to store:

Environment variables

While we make the request, we have no access to the result. There are a few different ways to get the result from a Promise, but we're going to use `async` and `await` to keep our code as clean and readable as possible. To get `async` and `await` working, we need to modify our handler function slightly. Where we have declared the input values, we need to declare that this function is an `async` function. We also need to check that our Lambda is running node 8.10 so it supports `async` functions. If you are using the build script that we created in Chapter 2, *Getting Started with AWS and Amazon CLI*, then all of our functions are automatically set up using node 8.10, but you can always check by looking at the runtime on your Lambda Console. We make our handle method asynchronous by adding `async` before the method name:

```
async handle(handlerInput) {}
```

To get the results from a promise using `async` and `await`, we need to put an `await` before the promise. This means that the rest of the code won't start running until the promise has returned:

```
let result = await promise();
```

Now that we've had a quick introduction to `axios` and `async/await`, we can start writing the requests that we are going to make. Because we have different URLs for *current weather* and *weather forecast*, we need to check whether the date selected is the current date or whether they are looking for a forecast.

Comparing dates is a surprisingly complicated task, so we are going to use an `npm` package to make it much easier. This package is called `moment`, and it is a package that is made to work with dates. Install it to our Lambda using `npm install --save moment` and then require it into Lambda by adding `const moment = require('moment');` `moment().format();` to the top of our `index.js` file.

Back in `handler`, we can add the following check:

```
let isToday = moment(date).isSame(Date.now(), 'day');

if (isToday) {
    // lookup todays weather
} else {
    // lookup forecast
}
```

Next, we need to add in the request that we are going to make to `openWeatherMaps`. The response that we get from `axios` is all of the information about the request. Because we only care about the data that is returned, we can destructure the response and rename the data. Destructuring allows us to select a key from an object and name it as something else:

```
let { key: newKeyName } = { key: 'this is some data' };
```

We can use this destructuring to rename the current weather data and forecast data differently, to avoid future confusion:

```
if (isToday) {
    let { data: weatherResponse } = await
axios.get(`https://api.openweathermap.org/data/2.5/weather?q=${location},us
&&appid=${process.env.API_KEY}`);
} else {
    let { data: forecastResponse } = await
axios.get(`https://api.openweathermap.org/data/2.5/forecast?q=${location},u
s&&appid=${process.env.API_KEY}`);
}
```

With the responses from these requests, we need to extract the information that we want to send to the user. For this, we need to know the data that we're going to receive and the data we want at the end.

One great way to check the exact data you will receive is to make test requests to the API. A great tool for making API requests is `Postman`, as it allows you to make `GET`, `PUT`, `POST`, and `DELETE` requests and see the results. To test our API request, we can open Postman and put `https://api.openweathermap.org/data/2.5/weather?q={$location},us,&APPID=${API_KEY}` into the request bar. Before making the request, just change `${location}` to be a test city and `${API_KEY}` to be the API key that we generated on the Open Weather Map website. It should look something like this: `https://api.openweathermap.org/data/2.5/weather?q=manchester,us,&APPID=12345678`.

From this request, we will get a result similar to this:

```
{
    "coord": {
        "lon": -71.45,
        "lat": 43
    },
    "weather": [
        {
            "id": 500,
            "main": "Rain",
            "description": "light rain",
            "icon": "10n"
        },
        {
            "id": 701,
            "main": "Mist",
            "description": "mist",
            "icon": "50n"
        }
    ],
    "base": "stations",
    "main": {
        "temp": 283.98,
        "pressure": 1016,
        "humidity": 93,
        "temp_min": 282.15,
        "temp_max": 285.15
    },
    "visibility": 16093,
    "wind": {
        "speed": 1.21,
```

```
        "deg": 197
    },
    "clouds": {
        "all": 90
    },
    "dt": 1526794800,
    "sys": {
        "type": 1,
        "id": 1944,
        "message": 0.0032,
        "country": "US",
        "sunrise": 1526807853,
        "sunset": 1526861265
    },
    "id": 5089178,
    "name": "Manchester",
    "cod": 200
}
```

From this data, the information that we are likely to want to tell the user will come from the weather and the main sections, with the rest of the data being less relevant for us. To remove this information, we can use destructuring again:

```
let { weather, main: { temp, humidity } } = weatherResponse;
```

We need to do the same for the forecast requests. The data is different, so we will need to do a bit more processing to extract the data we want:

```
let { list } = forecastResponse;
let usefulForecast = list.map(weatherPeriod => {
    let { dt_txt, weather, main: { temp, humidity } } = weatherPeriod;
    return  { dt_txt, weather, temp, humidity }
});
```

We now have forecast data for every three hours for the next five days. This is too much data to try to tell a user, even if they are only asking for a single day. To cut the data down, we can reduce the forecast to one at 9:00 and one at 18:00. We can use a filter on the usefulForecast array so that the dt_txt has to end at 09:00:00 or 18:00:00:

```
let reducedForecast = usefulForecast.filter(weatherPeriod => {
    let time = weatherPeriod.dt_txt.slice(-8);
    return time === '09:00:00' || time === '18:00:00';
});
```

We can now get the two forecasts for the day that the user requested. We can use moment again to compare the results and the date selected by the user:

```
let dayForecast = reducedForecast.filter(forecast => {
    return moment(date).isSame(forecast.dt_txt, 'day');
});
```

We should now have an array that contains two forecasts with the weather, temperature, and humidity for 9:00 and 18:00 on the day the user asked about.

With the data for the current weather and forecasts, we can start to create the user response. We'll start with a current weather request. We can use template strings to make the formatting easy. You can modify the phrasing or the structure all that you want, as long as you use the correct variables:

```
let speechText = `The weather in ${location} has ${weatherString} with a
temperature of ${formattedTemp} and a humidity of ${humidity} percent`;
```

You have probably noticed that we used two variables that we haven't defined yet. Let's look into that.

The weatherString needs to be made from the array of weather types that are currently happening. To deal with these, we can create a new function that takes the weather array and returns a string that is more human-/Alexa-readable. This function should be placed outside of the handlers object as a new function declaration:

```
const formatWeatherString = weather => {
    if (weather.length === 1) return weather[0].description
    return weather.slice( 0, -1 ).map( item => item.description ).join(',
') + ' and ' + weather.slice(-1)[0].description;
}
```

If there is only one weather type, this function returns the description. When there is more than one weather type, insert a comma between the types, apart from the last one, where it uses and to add it on. This would create strings such as *broken clouds, light rain and mist.*

Next, we need to convert the temperature into a scale that more people understand. The temperature we're given is in Kelvin, so we need to convert it to Celsius or Fahrenheit. I have provided the functions for both, but we only need to use one in our Lambda:

```
const tempC = temp => Math.floor(temp - 273.15) + ' degrees Celsius ';
```

```
const tempF = temp => Math.floor(9/5 *(temp - 273) + 32) + ' Fahrenheit';
```

Back inside our `getWeather` handler, we can now add the calls to these functions to our `isToday` if block. You can comment out the temperature function you don't want to use:

```
let weatherString = formatWeatherString(weather);
let formattedTemp = tempC(temp);
// let formattedTemp = tempF(temp);
```

Now that we have everything that we need to create the `speechText` variable that will be passed to the user, we need to follow a similar set of steps for the forecast data. We can start with the phrase that we want to build, which is a bit longer and more complex than the first one:

```
let speechText = ` The weather in ${location} ${date} will have
${weatherString[0]} with a temperature of ${formattedTemp[0]} and a
humidity of ${humidity[0]} percent, whilst in the afternoon it will have
${weatherString[1]} with a temperature of ${formattedTemp[1]} and a
humidity of ${humidity[1]} percent`
```

To populate these variables, we need to use the format `formatWeatherString()` and `tempC()` functions on both elements in the `dayForecast` array. You can switch `tempC()` for `tempC()` if you want to use Fahrenheit:

```
let weatherString = dayForecast.map(forecast =>
formatWeatherString(forecast.weather));
let formattedTemp = dayForecast.map(forecast => tempC(forecast.temp));
let humidity = dayForecast.map(forecast => forecast.humidity);
```

This will put the morning forecasts into the first index of the arrays as we required in our `speechText` string.

Now that we have the string responses for current weather and forecasts, we need to tell the user:

```
return handlerInput.responseBuilder
    .speak(speechText)
    .getResponse();
```

Once we save this function, we are ready to deploy this Lambda. With our build script, this is done by navigating into the main Lambda folder and running `./build.sh weatherGods`.

# Final setup and testing

With the Lambda created and uploaded, we can finish the last steps of the setup and then test out our skill. There are two things that we need to do before the skill starts working:

- Add **Alexa Skills Kit** as a trigger to the Lambda
- Add the **Lambda ARN** to the skill endpoint

We've done this all twice before, so this will be a brief guide. Open the Lambda Console and navigate into the `weatherGods` Lambda. In the **Designer** section, add the **Alexa Skills Kit** as a trigger and then add the **Skill ID** to the configuration window, and save the Lambda. Copy the **ARN** of the Lambda and navigate into the **Alexa Skills Kit Developer Console**, where we can go into the `WeatherGods` skill and add the **Lambda ARN** to the skill endpoint.

Now that the setup of the skill is done, we get to test it. In the Alexa Skill Kit console, make sure you are in the `WeatherGods` skill and that all of the items on the **Skill builder checklist** are complete. If you have any missing, then go back and complete that section:

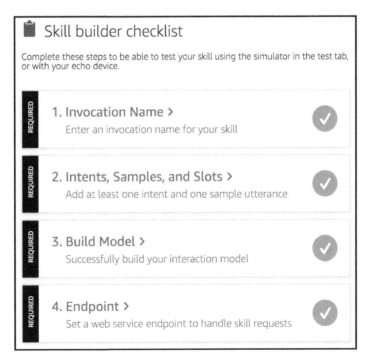

Skill-building checklist

Now we can go into the **Test** tab and try out this skill. We can start this skill and then ask for a forecast, and we should be told the forecast for a given city:

City forecast

This is a great place to try out different ways of asking the same thing and expanding the utterances for the intents.

# Improving user experience

While our first version of this skill works well, it can be improved in a few key sections.

- Error-handling
- Session memory
- SSML

# Error-handling our API calls

When we first set up this function, we didn't include any error-handling for our API calls. There is a chance that something happens with the API or with our call that causes it to fail. This could be a huge list of things such as broken internet connection, incorrect request, unknown location, expired API key, or the API going down.

To deal with this, we need to modify the way that our skill makes that request to the Open Weather Maps API. One of the limitations of using pure `async` and `await` is that we can't tell whether the request has passed or failed. There are two ways to deal with this:

1. You can use `try...catch` blocks to catch any errors that occur. The way that we would do this would be to wrap everything inside the `isToday` block in a `try` block and then have a `catch` that tells the user that we couldn't deal with the request.
2. You can pass the request to a function that returns an array of `[error, result]`. If no error occurs, then it will be `null` so we can do logic based on that fact.

Both of these methods are suitable, but they are best used in different situations.

The first `try...catch` method is used to catch errors across the code. We can take advantage of this by wrapping most of our logic in a single `try...catch`:

```
try {
    if (isToday) {
        ...
    } else {
        ...
    }
} catch (err) {
    console.log('err', err);
    return handlerInput.responseBuilder
        .speak(`My powers are weak and I couldn't get the weather right
now.`)
        .getResponse();
}
```

Keeping error messages light-hearted is often a good idea, as the user is less likely to be annoyed.

The second method is often used when you want to catch when a specific promise errors. We need to create a new function that takes a promise and returns the error and result status. This function is usually called `to`:

```
const to = promise => promise.then(res => [null, res]).catch(err => [err,
null]);
```

If this function gets a promise that resolves, it returns the error as `null` and the result. But if there is an error, it returns an error and a `null` result. The error always goes in the first position because of a standard design called **error-first programming**.

This method is good for catching errors at a very specific location, whether it is to handle it differently or just to log out more information at that point. We can use this on the current weather request to give a slightly different response:

```
let [error, response] = await
to(axios.get(`https://api.openweathermap.org/data/2.5/weather?q=${location}
,us&appid=${process.env.API_KEY}`));
if (error) {
 console.log('error getting weather', error.response);
    let errorSpeech = `We couldn't get the weather for ${location} but you
can try again later`;
    return handlerInput.responseBuilder
        .speak(errorSpeech)
        .getResponse();
}
let { data: weatherResponse } = response;
```

The last tool that we can use to handle errors is providing an error handler to the whole Alexa skill. We can create another handler that is called whenever there is an uncaught error in our code. This could be us returning an incorrect response, having an undefined variable, or an uncaught promise rejection.

Because we want this to be called every time an error occurs, our `canHandle` function always returns true. Our handler then gets passed the `handlerInput` but also gets passed an `error` variable. We can `console.log` out the response from the error and then send the user an error message:

```
const ErrorHandler = {
    canHandle() {
        return true;
    },
    handle(handlerInput, error) {
        console.log(`Error handled: ${error.message}`);

        return handlerInput.responseBuilder
```

```
                .speak(`Sorry, I can't understand the command. Please sa
    again.`)
                .getResponse();
        },
    };
```

To apply this handler to our skill, we can add `.addErrorHandlers(ErrorHandler)` after `.addRequestHandlers` in our `Alexa.SkillBuilders`.

With these measures in place, our skill will work much better if there is ever an error in our code or when making a request to the Open Weather Map API. You should always have some sort of error-handling process around API calls, as you never know when they might go wrong.

# Session memory

One thing that doesn't currently work is asking follow-up questions. From the initial perfect conversation, we had to follow up questions such as *What about tomorrow?* and *What about in Miami?* that use knowledge about previous requests to populate either the date or the location. Having a skill that can remember certain bits of information between interactions means that it can interact in a much more human way. There are very few interactions that we make that never depend on previous information.

To maintain that information between interactions, we have the concept of **session attributes**. These are key value pairs that are attached to the session, not just the individual interaction. Once Alexa thinks she's completed a task, she closes the session. In Alexa, session attributes are also really easy to set and retrieve. Getting session attributes is as simple as calling the following:

```
let sessionAttributes =
handlerInput.attributesManager.getSessionAttributes();
```

This means that we have access to the values that we have previously stored in session attributes. To store values in session attributes, we can pass an object into `.setSessionAttributes`:

```
handlerInput.attributesManager.setSessionAttributes(sessionAttributes);
```

The last thing that we need to do is to tell Alexa that the session hasn't finished yet. We do this by adding `.withShouldEndSession(false)` just before `.getResponse()` in our response builder when we want to keep the session attributes.

If the user doesn't respond within a set time, the session still gets closed:

```
return handlerInput.responseBuilder
    .speak(speechText)
    .withShouldEndSession(false)
    .getResponse();
```

We can use this powerful tool to store the date and location of successful requests and then use them to fill location or date slots that aren't filled by the user.

The first thing that we need to do is to get the session attributes from storage. We can then use these values to populate the `date` and `location` variables. If we don't get a value from the slots, we try the session attributes; otherwise, we set them to `null`. We then set out the local `sessionAttributes` variable to equal our `date` and `location`. This means that new values that come from slots override the existing session attribute values:

```
let sessionAttributes =
handlerInput.attributesManager.getSessionAttributes();
location = location.value || sessionAttributes.location || null;
date = date.value || sessionAttributes.date || null;
sessionAttributes = { location, date };
```

We have changed the local session attributes, but we haven't set them on the session yet. We leave this until just before we respond to the user. We choose not to save it straight away, as if the user provided an invalid slot, that would get stored. If we store it just before sending the message, then we know that the API calls have succeeded:

```
let speechText = `The weather in ${location} has ${weatherString} with a
temperature of ${formattedTemp} and a humidity of ${humidity} percent`;
handlerInput.attributesManager.setSessionAttributes(sessionAttributes);
return handlerInput.responseBuilder
```

Similarly, we need to add `handlerInput.attributesManager.setSessionAttributes(sessionAttributes);` just before returning the forecast message.

This example makes good use of session attributes, but it can be used for so much more. It can be used to store information for certain intents, previous conversation topics, or information about the user.

One thing to note is that session attributes only last as long as the conversation session with the user. If you want to maintain attributes from one session to another, you can use persistent attributes, but this involves configuring your skill with a **Persistence Adapter**. More details are available at the end of the chapter.

# SSML

When you are sending a response to a user, you may not want Alexa to say it in her normal way. Alexa is already pretty smart and handles punctuation, increasing the tone at the end of a question and pausing after a period, but what if you want to have greater control?

SSML is a standard markup for speech synthesis, and Alexa supports a subset of SSML, allowing the use of 13 different tags. These tags allow you to specify the way that the text is spoken. This means you can add `<break time="2s">` into your speech to add a two-second pause, emphasise a section of the speech using `<emphasis level="moderate">text to emphasise</emphasis>`, or `<prosody rate="slow" pitch="-2st">to change the tone and speed, </prosody>`, of the speech.

There are lots of ways to change the way that Alexa talks, and they can all be found in the Alexa SSML reference page (`https://developer.amazon.com/docs/custom-skills/speech-synthesis-markup-language-ssml-reference.html#emphasis`).

The speech that we are saying to the user is already handled very well because of Alexa's handling of punctuation and questions. This means there isn't much of our existing messages we could improve with SSML. To give us something that always needs extra speech control, we're going to add a new intent—`tellAJoke`. If you've ever heard someone ruin a good joke, then you know that jokes need proper tone, speed, and timing.

We need to add the `tellAJoke` intent in the Alexa Skills Kit console and then add a few utterances, but this time we don't need any slots.

Once we've saved and built the model, we can move back to our code to handle this new intent:

Intents / tellAJoke

Sample Utterances (4)

What might a user say to invoke this intent?

tell me another one

tell me a weather joke

make me laugh

tell me a joke

Adding the tell-a-joke intent

The handler for this intent is very simple. All that it needs to do is to get a random joke from the array of jokes and tell that to the user. We use `Math.floor(Math.random() * 3);` to get a random integer that is less than 3. If you want to add more jokes, just change 3 to the number of jokes you have:

```
const JokeHandler = {
    canHandle(handlerInput) {
        return handlerInput.requestEnvelope.request.type ===
'IntentRequest' &&
            handlerInput.requestEnvelope.request.intent.name ===
'tellAJoke';
    },
    async handle(handlerInput) {
        let random = Math.floor(Math.random() * 3);
        let joke = jokes[random];
        return handlerInput.responseBuilder
            .speak(joke)
            .getResponse();
    }
};
```

The more interesting part is creating the jokes. We need to start by creating a variable called `jokes` that is an array. Inside this array, we can put a few weather-related jokes. I've added the first three, but feel free to add your own (and remove my less-funny ones):

```
let jokes = [
    `Where do snowmen keep their money? In a snow bank.`,
    `As we waited for a bus in the frosty weather, the woman next to me
mentioned that she makes a lot of mistakes when texting in the cold. I
nodded knowingly. It's the early signs of typothermia.`,
    `Don't knock the weather. If it didn't change once in a while, nine
tenths of the people couldn't start a conversation.`
];
```

If we published the skill now, those jokes would be even worse than they're meant to be. The first thing that we will aim to fix will be the timing. Adding break tags before the punchline makes the jokes far better:

```
let jokes = [
    `Where do snowmen keep their money? <break time="2s" /> In a snow
bank.`,
    `As we waited for a bus in the frosty weather, the woman next to me
mentioned that she makes a lot of mistakes when texting in the cold. I
nodded knowingly. <break time="1s" /> It's the early signs of typothermia.`,
    `Don't knock the weather. <break time="1s" /> If it didn't change once in
a while, nine tenths of the people couldn't start a conversation.`
];
```

The exact timings may not be perfect, but they're already delivered much better than before. Another key to telling a joke well is the emphasis you place on certain words. Adding emphasis to sections of speech in Alexa is done by wrapping those words in `emphasis` tags:

```
`This sentence uses both <emphasis level="strong">increased</emphasis> and
<emphasis level="reduced">decreased</emphasis> emphasis`;
```

Adding `emphasis` tags to our jokes, we get this:

```
let jokes = [
    `Where do snowmen keep their money? <break time="2s" /> In a <emphasis>
snow bank </emphasis>`,
    `As we waited for a bus in the frosty weather, the woman next to me
mentioned that she makes a lot of mistakes when texting in the cold. I
nodded knowingly. <break time="1s" /> It's the early signs of <emphasis>
typothermia </emphasis>`,
```

```
    `Don't knock the weather. <break time="1s" /> If it didn't change once in
a while, nine tenths of the people <emphasis> couldn't start a
conversation</emphasis>`
];
```

When the `emphasis` tags are used but a level is not provided, a level of *moderate* is used.

There are lots of other SSML tags that can be used to alter the way that Alexa says the response, and they can be found on the Alexa SSML page (`https://developer.amazon. com/docs/custom-skills/speech-synthesis-markup-language-ssml-reference.html`).

# Testing

Now that we've added all of these changes to our Lambda, we can build it and test it out.

It's quite hard to test what happens when API errors occur, but we can test for session attributes and SSML.

Session attributes can be tested by asking to follow up questions, where we expect that some data has been stored from the last question. We can ask for a forecast in one location, and then ask for a new location. The date should have been saved in session attributes, so we should get a forecast for the new location instead of the current weather. We can then ask about today's weather, and the new location should have been saved, so we shouldn't get prompted for the location:

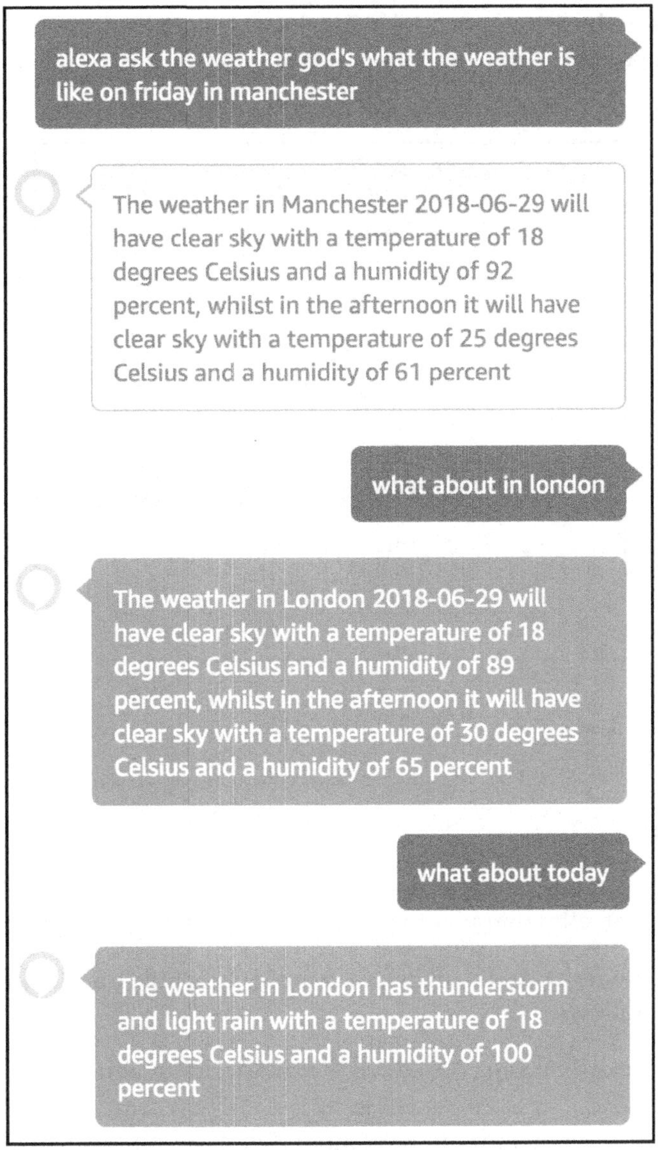

alexa ask the weather god's what the weather is like on friday in manchester

The weather in Manchester 2018-06-29 will have clear sky with a temperature of 18 degrees Celsius and a humidity of 92 percent, whilst in the afternoon it will have clear sky with a temperature of 25 degrees Celsius and a humidity of 61 percent

what about in london

The weather in London 2018-06-29 will have clear sky with a temperature of 18 degrees Celsius and a humidity of 89 percent, whilst in the afternoon it will have clear sky with a temperature of 30 degrees Celsius and a humidity of 65 percent

what about today

The weather in London has thunderstorm and light rain with a temperature of 18 degrees Celsius and a humidity of 100 percent

Session attributes testing

We can also test SSML by asking for a joke. The joke you get back should have the break that we added and possibly some emphasis. When you test this yourself, you will be able to hear these clearly:

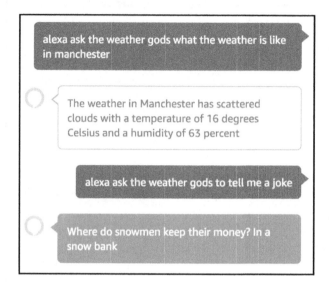

alexa ask the weather gods what the weather is like in manchester

The weather in Manchester has scattered clouds with a temperature of 16 degrees Celsius and a humidity of 63 percent

alexa ask the weather gods to tell me a joke

Where do snowmen keep their money? In a snow bank

Jokes

# Summary

In this chapter, we've covered how to use external APIs to increase the information that is available to the chatbot, allowing you to make much more powerful skills.

We then looked at how to make the experience more enjoyable for the user. The three ways we did this were as follows:

- We used error-handling to reduce the frustration when a user's request doesn't work.
- We used session memory to remember details about the conversation so that we can use them later. This stopped us from repeating and prompting the user every time they didn't provide all of the information.
- We used SSML to modify the way that Alexa says our responses, to make the sentence feel more human. We also used SSML to make jokes funnier, but it can be used to emphasize points or change the tone of the speech.

# Questions

1. What is an API?
2. How does Axios differ from the standard HTTP request library?
3. What are the two common ways of handling `async` and `await` errors?
4. How would we store *color* on the session attributes?
5. What types of data can be stored on the session attributes?
6. Why would you use SSML?

# Further reading

If you want to learn about *persistentAttributes*, then you can read about them in the ASK SDK documents (`https://ask-sdk-for-nodejs.readthedocs.io/en/latest/Managing-Attributes.html`).

For a full list of the supported SMML tags in Alexa, go to the Alexa SSML reference page (`https://developer.amazon.com/docs/custom-skills/speech-synthesis-markup-language-ssml-reference.html`).

If you want to hear how different SSML tags change the way that text is spoken, check out the Google SSML reference page (`https://developers.google.com/actions/reference/ssml`). It has working examples of lots of SSMLs, but you can't edit them.

# Building Your First Amazon Lex Chatbot

**5**

The preceding two chapters focused solely on Amazon Alexa and building Alexa Skills. The next three chapters will teach you how to build chatbots using Amazon Lex. In this chapter, we'll learn how to build and test a Lex chatbot and then we'll step things up by integrating S3.

Amazon Lex is very similar to Amazon Alexa but the main difference is that Lex has been designed to primarily work as a typed interaction. This means that you can use Lex to power Facebook messenger bots, add functionality to Slack, or even send text messages to your users. This doesn't stop you from using Lex for voice interactions and it can be used to build voice-based chatbots outside of the Amazon Alexa ecosystem.

The following topics will be covered in this chapter:

- Creating a Lex chatbot with slots and built-in responses
- Creating an FAQ chatbot with Lambda fulfillment
- Retrieving answers from S3 storage

## Technical requirements

In this chapter, we will be creating a Lambda function for our skill, and we'll be creating and deploying it using the local development setup that we created in Chapter 2, *Getting Started with AWS and Amazon CLI*.

All of the code and data required for this chapter can be found at http://bit.ly/chatbot-ch5.

# Creating an Amazon Lex chatbot

Creating a Lex chatbot is very similar to the process of creating an Alexa skill. We need to create intents with utterances, we can have slots with slot types on those intents, and we can then build a response to the user. Although Lex and Alexa are very similar, there are some key differences that we will look at as we go through this chapter.

## Setting up the chatbot

To start creating our first Lex chatbot, we need to open the AWS console and search for *Lex*. Once on the Lex page, click **Get Started** to get to the bot setup page. You'll be presented with the option to use one of three sample bots or to create a **Custom bot**. We'll be creating a custom bot, so select that option. The other three options are sample bots. These have been built to showcase the applications that you can use a Lex chatbot for:

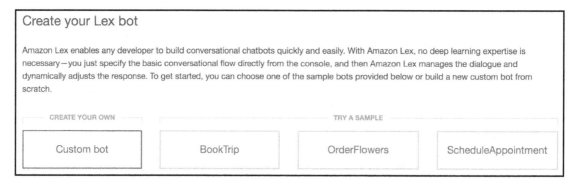

Bot-creation options

Having selected **Custom bot**, we get to name our bot and set up a few other settings. All of these settings are editable later, so we can start with some defaults.

Select a voice for your chatbot. This is the voice that will be used if you want to set up your Lex bot for voice-based chatbots. As we are going to be using Lex for text-based interactions only, we could select **None.** We'll be building a text-based application, but you should still choose a voice so you can test with voice.

The last two parts are to set a timeout; we can use the default of **5** minutes, and select **No** for the **COPPA** question. If you want to create a chatbot that will talk with children, ticking **Yes** will stop Lex from storing any of the conversations to comply with the Children's Online Privacy Protection Act. Now that we've finished the settings, we can click **Create**. This takes us to the Lex dashboard:

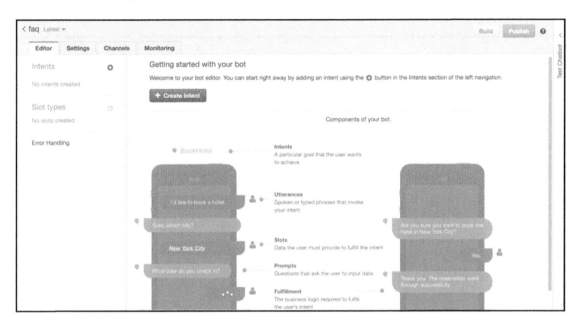

Lex dashboard

The components and process of creating a Lex chatbot are very similar to the process of creating an Alexa skill. There are **Intents**, **Utterances**, **Slots**, and **Slot types**, and the creation of most of these is almost identical to their creation in Alexa.

# Creating an Intent

The first thing we want to do is **Create intent**. Unlike Alexa, we have the option to **Create intent**, **Import intent**, or **Search existing intents**. As this is our first intent in Lex, we need to **Create intent**. We are prompted for a name for our new intent; we should call our first intent `sayHello`:

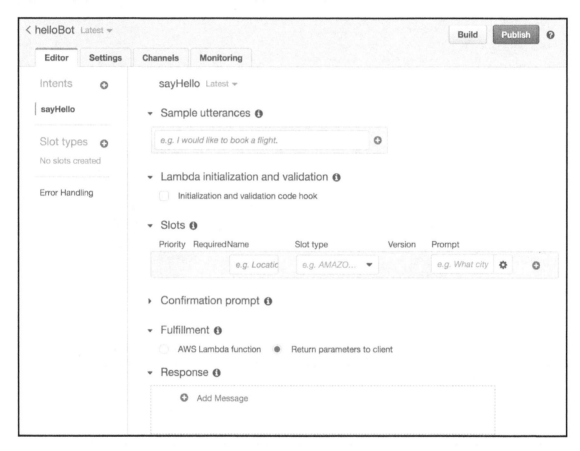

Intent screen

First, we need to add utterances so that the user can trigger the intent. We can add the utterances of `hi`, `hey`, and `hello`. These are not case-sensitive, and adding punctuation such as commas and full stops is unnecessary, although apostrophes are accepted.

One of the biggest differences between Lex and Alexa is that we can send responses without needing a Lambda. Scroll to the bottom of the page and you will see the **Fulfillment** and **Response** sections. The **Fulfillment** section lets you decide whether to send this intent to a Lambda. For now, we are going to keep that option on **Return parameters to client**.

Inside the **Response** section is where we can tell Lex what to send back to the user. Click the **Add Message** button and a message block will appear. In the text area, we can type the response we want to send back to the user. Add a response phrase such as `Hi there` and press *Enter*. Unlike the utterances, the response is case-sensitive and can contain any punctuation you want:

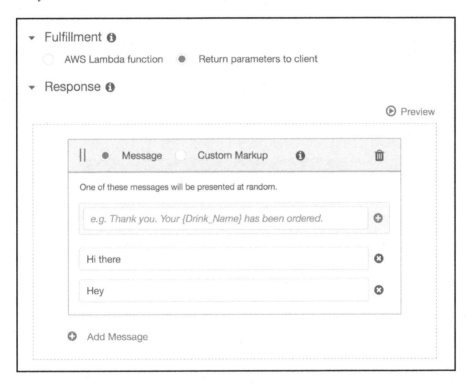

Fulfillment and response

We can actually add multiple response messages, and Lex will choose one of them at random. This makes multiple interactions with the chatbot feel more natural and less robotic.

With the utterances and the response completed, we can save the intent with the **Save Intent** button at the bottom of the intent. Once that has saved, we can build our bot.

Building the bot takes all of the utterances from your intents and adds them to a language model. Click the **Build** button in the upper-right corner of the screen and wait for the system to put the bot together.

# Testing your chatbot

When Lex has finished building, you will get a notification and a new **Test bot** section will open on the right of your screen. This is a basic text chat interface where you can try out your bot. Try typing Hi into the chat and you should get a response of **Hi there** or **Hey**:

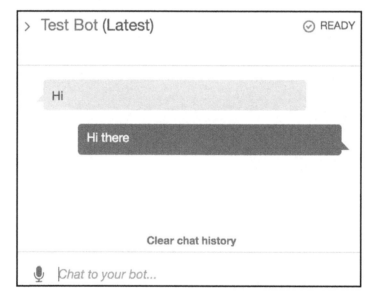

Initial test

If you don't, check that you have added the utterances and responses, and rebuild the chatbot.

You can also test your bot by speaking to it. Click the microphone symbol, say Hello, and then click the microphone again. You should see what you said, and get a spoken response as well as a text response. If you get an error about not having a selected voice, go to **Settings** | **General** and change the output voice.

# Publishing your bot

With a working chatbot, we can publish the bot. Clicking the **Publish** button opens a popup where we can select the alias that we want to publish to. This is useful when you want to test that a new version of the bot is fully functional without replacing the existing live version. You can create a **development** or **test** alias without overwriting the existing **production** bot:

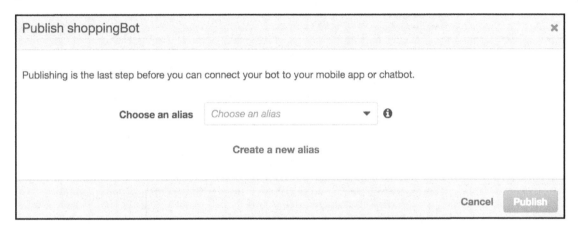

Publishing your bot

Once the **Publish** is complete, you can access this new alias from other services.

# Using Slots

As we saw with Alexa, having a set response is OK, but using slots to customize the interaction is much better. Go into the **sayHello** intent screen and scroll down to **Slots**. This is identical to the slot configuration in Alexa.

Give a name to the slot you want to get; in this case, we can ask them for their name so we call the slot usersName. We have to select a slot type and we can choose either **GB_FIRST_NAME** or **US_FIRST_NAME**. The last thing we need to do is to configure the prompt. Enter a question that will get them to enter their name, such as What is your name?. To add this slot, we need to click the blue plus button at the end of the line.

When we see the new line created, we can check that the **Required** checkbox is ticked so Lex knows to ask the user for this slot:

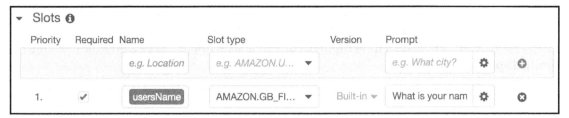

Slot creation

Now that we have a slot, we need to use the answer in our response. To add the slot into a response, we can wrap the slot name in curly braces. This means our response becomes `Hi there {usersName}`.

We can now save this intent again and rebuild the chatbot. Now we get a slightly longer conversation:

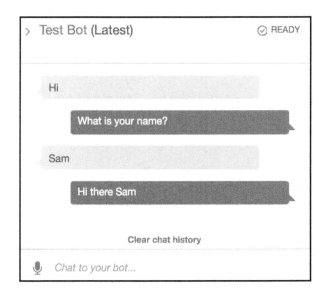

Test with name

# Creating an FAQ chatbot

Now that we've learned how to make a Lex chatbot, we can start to build something that you are more likely to see in the real world. FAQ chatbots are becoming more and more popular; they are relatively simple to create and are a great way to introduce a chatbot to a website or Facebook group.

To start creating an FAQ chatbot, we need to find an FAQ page to base this on. Most company websites have an FAQ page now so you can find the FAQ page for a company that interests you, or follow along with me on CircleLoop (`circleloop.com`). This site was chosen because it is where I work and it has the questions in three groups. If you are only doing this for practice, you can use any website, but if you want to publish your chatbot, ask the permission of the company. You never know, they could end up paying you for it eventually!

CircleLoop is also good as it has a total of 24 questions, which is a good amount – too many and it can take a very long time and Lex can mix up similar questions.

# Setting up Lex

As we did in the first half of this chapter, we need to create a new Lex chatbot. On the Lex console page there will be a list of all of your Lex chatbots, and above that will be a **Create** button.

Follow the same process as before, selecting **Custom bot**, naming your chatbot, choosing a voice, selecting a five-minute timeout, and selecting *No* for the COPPA question. If you are making a chatbot that is designed for children under 13, you should research COPPA and alter your answer accordingly.

# Gathering the data

All of the data files for this section are available at `https://bit.ly/chatbot-ch5` in the `data` folder, but if you are using your own company, you'll have to follow this process with your company's FAQs.

Before we start creating intents, we need to get the data that we will be using. Go to the **FAQ** page of your choice and open up a new file called `faq-setup.json`.

This file will contain a group of intents and answers in the following format:

```
{
     "intentName1": "This is the answer to question 1",
     "intentName2": "You do this by selecting 'A' and then pressing
'START'"
     ...
 }
```

The intent names should be unique strings that describe what the question is asking. For example, if you are asking, "Where is the company based?", you might call the intent `companyLocation`.

Go through all of the questions in the *Setting Up & Using CircleLoop* section of the site. Repeat the process with a new file for the *Users & Numbers* and *Other Questions* sections. You should end up with three JSON files that contain all of the answers on the website. Here is a section of one of the `faq-setup.json` files:

```
{
     "howItWorks": "CircleLoop is a cloud-based business phone system, which
allows ... settings.",
     "technicalKnowledge": "No. We've made it really easy with our simple
apps. As long as ... and you're ready to go.",
     ...
     "sevenDayTrial": "Full user privileges, including the ability to add
users ... during your trial period."
}
```

We are now going to upload these three files into an S3 bucket so that our Lambda functions can access them. In your AWS console, navigate to **S3** and click **Create bucket**. Give your bucket a unique name and continue through the configuration. We don't need to add any extra permissions to this bucket for this project:

Upload files

Now that we've created the bucket, we can upload our FAQ files. Click into your newly created bucket and then click the **Upload** button. Again, we don't need to change any of the permissions from their defaults.

# Creating the Intents

Once we've created and uploaded the JSON files, we need to create the intents to match up. Go through your JSON files and create a new intent for each line. The intent names need to be exactly the same as the keys in the JSON file object. You can then use the questions from the FAQ page as the first utterance for that intent:

Intents

By the end of this process, you should have as many intents as you do rows in your JSON files. You should then go through and add more utterances to each intent. These new utterances should be other ways to phrase the same question. Expanding the list of utterances increases the chance that the user will get the correct answer.

# Creating the Lambda Handler

Now that we have the intents—catching the user utterances—we need to create the responses to send to the user. Because we have three files, we can create three Lambdas.

Each Lambda will deal with questions about one section.

Create three folders in your main Lambda folder, called `CL-setup`, `CL-users`, and `CL-other`. Inside each of the folders, create an `index.js` file. Open up the `index.js` file inside `CL-setup` and we can start to program the handler, starting with an empty handler:

```
exports.handler = async event => {
};
```

First, we need to find out which intent triggered the Lambda. The structure of the data received from Lex is slightly different from the structure of the data received from Alexa:

```
let intentName = event.currentIntent.name;
```

Now that we have the intent name, we need to make a request to S3 to get the file that contains the answer. As we did in Chapter 3, *Creating Your First Alexa Skill,* we first need to require in AWS and create a new instance of S3. Add this code at the very top of the file, just before `exports.handler`:

```
const AWS = require('aws-sdk');
const s3 = new AWS.S3();
```

To make a request to S3, we need to pass in some query parameters. This is an object containing the `Bucket` that contains our object and the `Key` of the object we want.

Because we're using Node 8.10 and an `async` function, we need to return a promised value. This means we need to create a `new Promise` and then `resolve` and `reject` our results. Back inside our handler function, we can add this code. Unlike in Chapter 3, *Creating Your First Alexa Skill,* we can set `Key` to a fixed value of `faq-setup.json` for this Lambda, as this Lambda is only going to be called for questions from the *Set Up & Using CircleLoop* section:

```
var params = {
    Bucket: 'cl-faq',
    Key: `faq-setup.json`
};

return new Promise((resolve, reject) => {
    // do something
    resolve(success);
    reject(failure);
})
```

We can put our `s3.getObject()` code inside this `Promise`, resolving `handleS3Data()` and rejecting `handleS3Error()`:

```
return new Promise((resolve, reject) => {
    s3.getObject(params, function(err, data) {
        if (err) { // an error occurred
            reject(handleS3Error(err));
        } else { // successful response
            console.log(data);
            resolve(handleS3Data(data, intentName));
        }
    });
})
```

We now need to create the two handlers for the S3 responses. These functions can be created after the handler:

```
const handleS3Error = err => {
}

const handleS3Data = (data, intentName) => {
}
```

We will start by creating the data-handler. Inside here, we first need to parse the body of the data. This is because it comes down as a *buffer* that needs to be turned into JSON before we can work with it:

```
let body = JSON.parse(data.Body);
```

With the data in JSON format, we can now check that `intentName` is one of the keys in the object. If it isn't, we need to return the `handleS3Error` function to send the user an error message:

```
if (!body[intentName]){
    return handleS3Error(`Intent name ${intentName} was not present in faq-
setup.json`);
}
```

In `handleS3Error`, we can `console.log` the error and then create an error response string. This should tell the user there was an error and ask them to try asking another question:

```
console.log('error of: ', err);
let errResponse = `Unfortunately I don't know how to answer that. Is there
anything else I can help you with?`;
```

# Creating a response

The way that you create a response in Lex is very different from how it's done in Alexa. In Lex, there is an object structure that needs to be followed:

```
sessionAttributes: {},
dialogAction: {
    type: '',
    fulfillmentState: '',
    slots: {},
    slotToElicit: '',
    message: { contentType: 'PlainText', content:  ''};
}
```

Because this is a bit of code that we may use multiple times, we can create functions for each of the types. Here is a function for finishing the last stage of a conversation flow. This can be added to the bottom of the index.js file:

```
const lexClose = ({ message, sessionAttributes = {}, fulfillmentState =
"Fulfilled"}) => {
    return {
        sessionAttributes,
        dialogAction: {
            type: 'Close',
            fulfillmentState,
            message: { contentType: 'PlainText', content: message }
        }
    }
}
```

This function uses default values for sessionAttributes and fulfillmentState as we won't be setting either of them in most cases, but it is good to be able to if we wanted to.

With this new function, we can now create responses in our handler functions. Inside our handleS3Data function, we can return this lexClose function with the answer from the file as the message:

```
return lexClose({ message: body[intentName] });
```

We also need to make a lexElicitIntent function at the bottom of the file for when we tell the user to ask another question. This tells Lex that it should be expecting an intent utterance as its next message:

```
const lexElicitIntent = ({ message, sessionAttributes = {} } ) => {
    return {
        sessionAttributes,
        dialogAction: {
```

```
              type: 'ElicitIntent',
              message: { contentType: 'PlainText', content: message }
          },
      };
  }
```

This `lexElicitIntent` can then be returned at the end of the `handleS3Error` function to tell the user to ask another question:

```
  return lexElicitIntent({ message: errResponse });
```

This file can be copied into the other two folders. We only need to change `key` in the params object and the text in the error console log and response. With those changes made, we can deploy our three Lambdas using our build script.

With all three Lambdas deployed, we need to make sure their role includes permissions to access S3 buckets. Inside each of the Lambdas, scroll down to the **Role** section and we should be able to see the role of **lambdaBasic**. We should have updated this in Chapter 3, *Creating Your First Alexa Skill*, but we should check again. Navigate into the **IAM** service and make sure that **lambdaBasic** has S3 read permissions. If it doesn't, then attach **AmazonS3ReadOnlyAcess** to this role.

# Lambda fulfillment

We can use Lambdas to create the response of our intents. This gives us a lot more control than just having a text response. The great thing about Lex is that each intent can have its own Lambda handler or multiple intents can share one Lambda.

With the three Lambdas deployed, we can use them to fulfill the intents. We're going to have all of the intents about the setup share the `CL-setup` Lambda, all intents about users and numbers will share the `CL-users` Lambda, and all other questions will share the `CL-other` Lambda.

Open up your Lambda console and go into your FAQ chatbot. Open an intent and scroll down to the **Fulfillment** section.

There are two options:

- **AWS Lambda function**
- **Return parameters to client**

As we've created the Lambdas, we can select **AWS Lambda function**, which opens more menu items for us to select. The main one is the **Lambda** dropdown where we can select which Lambda will be triggered on the intent fulfillment:

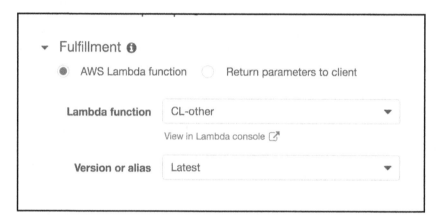

Intent fulfillment options

With the Lambda selected, we need to save the intent and move on to the next intent. This needs to be done for every intent in the chatbot, making sure to send the correct intents to the correct Lambdas.

# Building and testing

With all of the intents pointing to a fulfillment Lambda, we can build our chatbot and then test it. Click the **Build** button in the upper-right corner of the screen and wait until the build process has stopped. This may take a few minutes, and the *Test* section will open when the build process ends.

To test our chatbot, type a question and you should receive the correct answer:

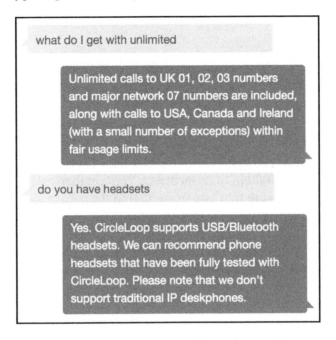

what do I get with unlimited

Unlimited calls to UK 01, 02, 03 numbers and major network 07 numbers are included, along with calls to USA, Canada and Ireland (with a small number of exceptions) within fair usage limits.

do you have headsets

Yes. CircleLoop supports USB/Bluetooth headsets. We can recommend phone headsets that have been fully tested with CircleLoop. Please note that we don't support traditional IP deskphones.

FAQ tests

If you don't get the correct answer, or don't get an error at all, then there are a few things to check:

- Look in the Lambda logs and check that the correct Lambda is being called. You should also be able to see a log with the error message, allowing you to pinpoint the error.
- Check that the Lambdas have permission to access the S3 buckets.
- Follow the Lambda debugging guide at the end of this book.

# Lex responses

We have just seen two of the different response types that can be returned to Lex. There are currently five different types of response that Lex can handle:

- `elicitSlot`
- `elicitIntent`

- confirmIntent
- close
- delegate

These can all be found at http://bit.ly/chatbot-ch5 in the All-Lex-Responses.js file. You can then copy them into your future projects.

# elicitSlot

The elicitSlot response type is very useful if you have been doing checks on your slot values and have found one of them to be incorrect. You can then ask the user to re-enter the value for that slot and make sure that Lex stores that in the correct slot.

To call elicitSlot, you need to pass in a message, the slots (an object containing all of the slots and current values), a slotToElicit value, and intentName:

```
const lexElicitSlot = ({ sessionAttributes = {}, message, intentName,
slotToElicit, slots }) => {
    return {
        sessionAttributes,
        dialogAction: {
            type: 'ElicitSlot',
            intentName,
            slots,
            slotToElicit,
            message: { contentType: 'PlainText', content: message }
        },
    };
}
```

If we rebuilt the car helper bot in Lex, we would use the lexElicitSlot function when we validate the slot values. If there was an incorrect slot, then we would call this function like so:

```
return lexElicitSlot({
    intentName: 'whichCar',
    slotToElicit: 'size',
    slots: {
        size: null,
        cost: 'value',
        doors: 5,
        gears: null
    }
})
```

# elicitIntent

We have already seen this Lex response, taking a message and session attributes. This is usually used to continue the conversation or to restart with a new intent:

```
const lexElicitIntent = ({ message, sessionAttributes = {} } ) => {
    return {
        sessionAttributes,
        dialogAction: {
            type: 'ElicitIntent',
            message: { contentType: 'PlainText', content: message }
        },
    };
}
```

# confirmIntent

The confirmIntent response is used when you want to ask a user whether they want to do something. This could be used at the end of the FAQ bot to ask Would you like to sign up?, which would be a confirmIntent response for a *signUp* intent. You need to pass in message, intentName, and the slots for that intent. Any slots that you don't want to pre-fill should have a value of null:

```
const lexConfirmIntent = ({ sessionAttributes = {}, intentName, slots,
message }) => {
    return {
        sessionAttributes,
        dialogAction: {
            type: 'ConfirmIntent',
            intentName,
            slots,
            message: { contentType: 'PlainText', content: message }
        },
    };
}
```

# close

This is the simplest and most-used Lex response. The only thing that you need to pass in is `message`:

```
const lexClose = ({ sessionAttributes = {}, fulfillmentState = 'Fulfilled',
message }) => {
    return {
        sessionAttributes,
        dialogAction: {
            type: 'Close',
            fulfillmentState,
            message: { contentType: 'PlainText', content: message }
        },
    };
}
```

# delegate

The `delegate` response is where you want to leave Lex to decide what to send to the user. This is most likely used if you have validated an input and you want Lex to ask for the next slot or move into fulfillment. It takes just a `slots` object that contains all of the slots for the current intent:

```
const lexDelegate = ({ sessionAttributes = {}, slots }) => {
    return {
        sessionAttributes,
        dialogAction: { type: 'Delegate', slots, }
    };
}
```

# Summary

This chapter has been an introduction to Amazon Lex. You've learned that Lex and Alexa are very similar in form and function, but there are a few differences in how they are built and how they work.

We can now create a Lex chatbot with intents, slots, and hardcoded responses. We can then increase the functionality by creating Lambdas to handle intent fulfillment. One advantage of Lex over Alexa is that we can use multiple Lambdas to handle different intents. To help us easily respond to Lex, we created a `Lex` class that maps values into the correct response format.

We used these skills to build an FAQ chatbot that gets data from S3 and uses that to generate a response.

In the next chapter we will take what we have learned in this chapter and build upon it by adding a database to our chatbot. We will use DynamoDB to store information about the chat, allowing us to make a more realistic chatbot conversation.

# Questions

1. Can you create a Lex chatbot without using Lambdas?
2. How do you include a slot in a response from Lex?
3. How does Lex use Lambdas differently from Alexa?
4. How many response types does Lex deal with?
5. Can you name them all?
6. What is the name of the function to get data from S3?

# 6
# Connecting a Lex Bot to DynamoDB

After reading the previous chapter, we know how to create a Lex chatbot. Now we can start building a chatbot that takes the user through a more complex flow. Designing and building larger chatbots is closer to what you are likely to be doing, and we'll look at the best ways to approach the design and setup.

We'll be using our chatbot to get data from S3 as well as getting and writing data to DynamoDB tables. This allows us to persist information about the users' choices and progress through the flow.

The following topics will be covered in this chapter:

- Creating flow diagrams for a larger, more complex chatbot
- Creating a Lex chatbot to cover all of the intents and flows
- Retrieving data from an S3 bucket and performing logic upon it
- Creating a Dynamo table and using it to store and retrieve information

## Technical requirements

In this chapter, we will be creating a Lambda function for our skill, and we'll be creating and deploying it using the local development setup that we created in Chapter 2, *Getting Started with AWS and Amazon CLI*.

All of the code and data required for this chapter can be found at http://bit.ly/chatbot-ch6.

# Designing the flows

The FAQ chatbot that we built in the previous chapter didn't need to have any flows designed as everything was simply a question and an answer. This chatbot will be a lot more complex, with multiple flows, some of which will lead to other intents and flows.

# Perfect conversations

As always, we can start to build flow diagrams by starting with perfect conversations. The difference this time is that we will have a few different conversations. We'll have some that go from asking about stock to making a purchase, others will stop before checking out, and some people won't even add anything to their basket. These are all flows that we will need to design and build.

It is good to start with a conversation that goes through the whole process. Here is one such conversation:

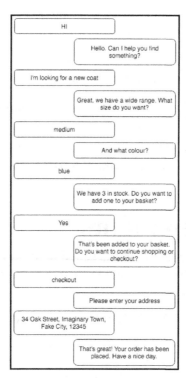

Full process conversation

We can also create other conversations that deal with part of the flow. A user could add some items to their basket and then save them for later, while another user will want to ask what is in their cart before checking out. You can probably see that some of these conversations will overlap. This will become more apparent as we progress onto our flow diagrams.

# Flow diagrams

As this is a large and complex conversation, we are going to break the flow into sections. This will make it easier to create and visualize.

The first part of the full conversation, as well as the stock-checking conversation, can be used to create a `productFind` flow diagram:

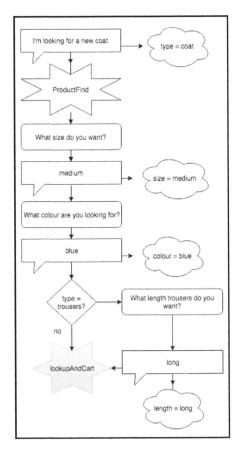

The productFind flow diagram

As you can see, there is some logic that is similar to the logic that we used in the Car Helper chatbot in Chapter 3, *Creating Your First Alexa Skill*. By the end of this flow, we know what product the user is asking about.

You may have noticed a new symbol in this flow. This symbol is similar to intentTrigger but this is for starting another flow. Breaking the whole flow into smaller chunks that can call each other is the best way to keep your diagrams organized:

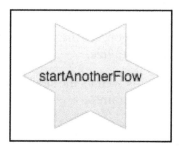

Start another flow

Now that we know what product the user is asking about, we can create a flow for checking stock and asking whether they want to add that to their cart. This starts with a request to S3, and if there is stock and they want it, we add it to their basket in Dynamo:

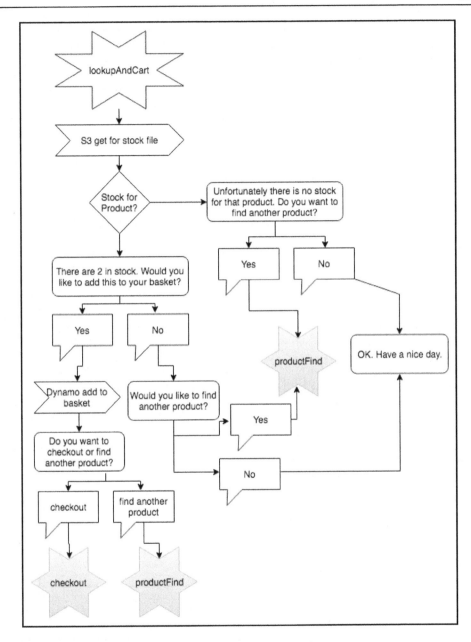

Stock and cart

The last stage of this conversation is the checkout. This is about getting a few details about the user so we can place the order. This would normally include taking a card payment, but we won't be doing that with this chatbot:

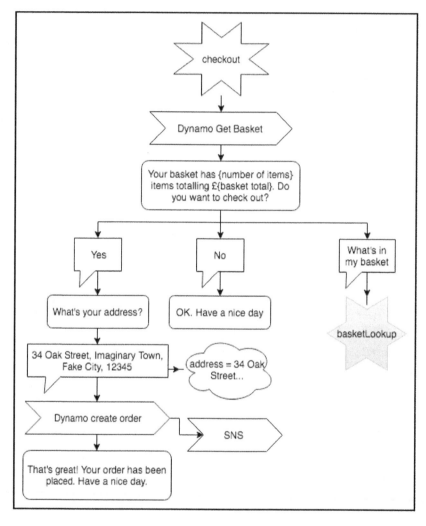

Checkout

The reason that we are breaking the conversation into multiple smaller flow diagrams is so that each flow does a single thing. This means that we can link different flows together. What if we have a user who knows the ID for the item? We can have them skip the productFind flow and start at the lookupAndCart flow.

When we consider a few other conversations, we end up with a web of flows in a master flow diagram:

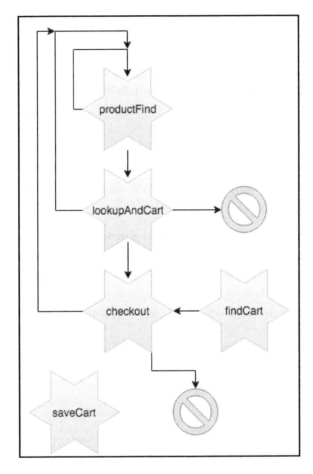

Master flow diagram

This master flow diagram shows how each of the sub-flows can be connected together to map any conversation. This web of conversation allows the chatbot to deal with the user in a much more human way than older chatbots that had a single path that the user had to follow.

# Building the chatbot

With all of the sub-flow diagrams and the master flow diagram, we can start to build the chatbot. Another great thing about having these sub-flows is that they are quite similar to intents.

Before we can start creating intents, we need to set up our Lex bot. In the Lex console, click **Create** and then follow the process for creating a **Custom bot** as described in `Chapter 5`, *Building Your First Amazon Lex Chatbot*.

# Product find

We will start with the most common conversation—finding a product. First, we'll create a new intent called `productFind`.

This intent will deal with users who want to find a product to add to their cart, as well as users just checking the stock levels, so we need to provide utterances to represent this. We also need to deal with user utterances such as, "I want a new jacket" and "Do you have any medium, blue shirts in stock?"

To capture the slot values from the utterances, we can use curly braces around the slot name:

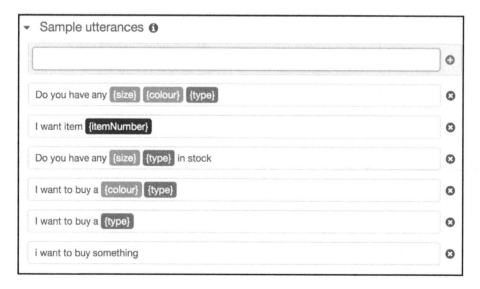

Utterances for productFind

With some utterances created, we need to create the slots and slot types. For the `productFind` intent, we need quite a few slots: `type`, `size`, `color`, `length`, and `itemNumber`. The first four are self-explanatory but `itemNumber` is less obvious.

We want to include an item number slot so that if a customer wants to buy a product that they already have, they don't need to go through the longer question-answer product-finding flow. These small things are what separate good bots from great bots.

Next, we need to choose a slot type for each of our slots. For the first four slots, we're going to need to create custom slots:

- **Type**: We are going to be selling three types of clothing: shirts, jackets, and trousers (pants).

  Click the **+** next to **Slot types** and choose **Create slot type**. Name your slot something such as `clothingType` and select **Restrict to Slot values and Synonyms**. It is a good idea to be relatively specific with your slot type naming as you can't have two slot types with the same name.

  We can now add our values of the shirt, jacket, and trousers. We then need to add synonyms that the user might type. Instead of `shirt`, they may type `blouse`, `top`, or `t-shirt`. For `trousers`, they might type `a pair of trousers`, `pants`, or `a pair of pants`. Expand all of the synonyms for all of the values until you can't think of anything else.

- **Size**: Size is going to be a very similar process to *type* with values of *large*, *medium*, and *small*. If this was for a genuine retailer, you'd have a lot more size options, and probably size options based on the type of item.

  Make sure to include some synonyms for each of the color values. We could use `AMAZON.Color` for the **color** but that would allow hundreds of colors through – to make our lives easier, we're going to have five colors.

  Create a custom slot type with the colors of *black*, *white*, *red*, *pink*, and *blue*. You can add synonyms of the colors, but it is more likely they are just saying a color we don't support.

  `Length`: **Length** has values of `long`, `standard`, and `short`. Make sure to add in any synonyms you can think of, such as `medium` and `normal` as synonyms for standard.

- **Item Number**: We don't need to create a new slot type for order numbers as we can use **AMAZON.NUMBER**. If we wanted to use item numbers, such as *SH429178*, where we use numbers and letters, we would have to use a custom slot type:

Competed slots

We need to change all of the slots to not be required. This is because if a user asks for an item by item number, we don't want to ask them about what size and color they want as the item has a size and color already.

# Creating the Lambda

The Lambda that handles this intent is going to need to do a few things:

- It needs to check whether it has an item number or all of the correct slots are filled.
- It then needs to get our S3 stock data and check the stock levels of the item requested.
- If there is stock, it will ask the user whether they want to add it to their cart. If there's no stock, it will tell the user and ask whether they want to find another product.

Start by creating a new folder in `Lambdas` called `productFind` and create an `index.js` file inside there. The `index.js` file can start with our default Node 8.10 handler and we will pass the event to a `handleProductFind` function:

```
exports.handler = async (event) => {
    return handleProductFind(event);
}
```

Inside this `handleProductFind` function, we start by checking the slot values. The first one to check is `itemNumber`, because if that one is present, we don't need any of the other slots. After that, we check the type, size, and color before finally checking the length if the type is `trousers`:

```
const handleProductFind = event => {
    let { slots } = event.currentIntent;
    let { itemNumber, type, size, colour, length } = slots;

    if (itemNumber) return getItem(slots);
    // No item number so using normal product find
    if (!type) {
        let message = 'Are you looking for a shirt, jacket or trousers?';
        let intentName = 'productFind';
        let slotToElicit = 'type';
        return Lex.elicitSlot({ message, intentName, slotToElicit, slots })
    }
    ...
}
```

We can copy the code for the `type` check and repeat it for the `size`, `color`, and `length` slots, changing just `message` and `slotToElicit` for each test. The `length` check needs to be modified further so that it also checks that `type` is `trousers`:

```
if ( !length && type === 'trousers' ){ ... }
```

After the last check, we can call a function to get the item that the user has chosen through their selections. We need to pass through the slots so that we can filter down the items by user choice:

```
return getItem(slots);
```

Inside our `getItem()` function we need to do three things: get the data, filter out just the item that matches the user answers, and create a response.

To get all of the stock data from S3, we are going to create a `getStock()` function. This is going to be the same as the S3 requests that we have made before. We can then call that as the first part of the `getItem()` function:

```
const getStock = () => {
    var params = {
        Bucket: 'shopping-stock',
        Key: `stock.json`
    };

    return new Promise((resolve, reject) => {
```

```
        s3.getObject(params, function(err, data) {
            if (err) { // an error occurred
                reject(err)
            } else { // successful response
                resolve(JSON.parse(data.Body).stock)
            }
        });
    })
}
```

We also need to require in `aws-sdk` and create an `s3` instance. In your folder, run `npm install --save aws-sdk`. Put this code at the top of the file:

```
const AWS = require('aws-sdk');
const s3 = new AWS.sS()'
```

Now that we have the data, we need to filter out the correct item. Arrays have a very useful function called `.find`. This function will go through each of the items in an array and run some code on that item. This will happen until an item returns `true` when the function returns the item that satisfied the function. If no item satisfied the function, `undefined` is returned.

We can use this to get the item that the user wants. We want to return `true` if all of the slots match the values on the item or the `itemNumber` matches. We also need to make sure that if the type is `trousers`, then the `length` matches as well:

```
let matching = stock.find(item =>
    itemNumber === item.itemNumber ||
    type == item.type &&
    size == item.size &&
    colour == item.colour &&
    (item.length == length || item.type != 'trousers'));
```

After this, we expect that we will have one item. If we don't, either we've created the function incorrectly or the data was wrong. Either way, we need to tell the user that we haven't managed to find the item that they were looking for:

```
if (!matching) {
    let message = `Unfortunately we couldn't find the item you were looking
for`;
    return Lex.Close({ message })
}
```

If we found an item but there is no stock, then we can tell the user and ask whether they would like to find another product. This means we will be using the `confirmIntent` Lex response. This response takes an `intentName`, a `message`, and a `slots` object containing all of the slots with values or `null`:

```
if (matching.stock < 1) {
    let message = `Unfortunately we don't have anything matching your
request in stock. Would you like to search again?`;
    let intentName = 'productFind';
    slots = { type: null, size: null, colour: null, length: null,
itemNumber: null };
    return Lex.confirmIntent({ intentName, slots, message })
}
```

If we find the product and there is stock, then we need to tell the user how many we have in stock. One tricky thing we have to deal with is the plurality of the types. If we find more than one *shirt*, they are called *shirts*; when a user has chosen *trousers*, we could either have one *pair of trousers* or multiple *pairs of trousers*. To avoid making the message string really complicated, we can make a function that takes the type and stock and returns the correct unit name:

```
const units = (type, stock) => {
    if (type === 'trousers') {
        return `pair${stock !== 1 ? 's': ''} of trousers`
    }
    return `${type}${stock !== 1 ? 's': ''}`;
}
```

This means that we can create a much neater message for the user. The message that we will be asking will be whether they want to add this item to their basket. We can use another `confirmIntent` response with an `intentName` of `addToBasket` with slots of `itemNumber`, which are set to `matching.itemNumber`:

```
let message = `There are ${matching.stock} ${matching.colour}
${units(matching.type, matching.stock)} in stock. Would you like to add one
to your basket?`;
let intentName = 'addToBasket';
slots = { itemNumber: matching.itemNumber };
return Lex.confirmIntent({ intentName, slots, message });
```

Throughout this Lambda, we have been using a lot of `Lex.something` responses. These are methods on the `Lex` class. To make these work, we need to create a new class called `Lex`, which contains all of the Lex responses we talked about in the previous chapter.

Create a new file called `LexResponses.js`, and inside we will create our class:

```
module.exports = class Lex {
    ElicitSlot({ sessionAttributes = {}, message, intentName, slotToElicit,
slots }) { ... }
    Close({ message, sessionAttributes = {}, fulfillmentState = "Fulfilled"
}) { ... }
    ElicitIntent({ message, sessionAttributes = {} }) { ... }
    confirmIntent({ sessionAttributes = {}, intentName, slots, message }) {
... }
    delegate({ sessionAttributes = {}, slots }) { ... }
}
```

The objects that we return from these methods can be found at the end of the previous chapter, or the complete `LexResponses.js` file can be found at `bit.ly/chatbot-ch6`.

We then need to require this class in this file and create a new instance of the class. At the top of our `productFind/index.js` file, add these two lines of code. The first line requires our `Lex` class from our `LexResponses` file, before the second line creates a new instance of this class:

```
const lex = require('./LexResponses');
const Lex = new lex();
```

Earlier in this Lambda, we wrote that if there is no stock, we ask the user whether they want to find another order using `confirmIntent`. This `confirmIntent` response will hit our same Lambda, but there will be a slightly different format to the call. We need to look for those different requests and handle them accordingly.

If the Lambda was called with `confirmIntent`, then `event.currentIntent.confirmationStatus` will have a value of `Confirmed` or `Denied`. If the user denied the question (said "no"), then we can give them a goodbye message and close the message. If they confirmed, we can let the process fall through to the `handleProductFind()` function. The following code needs to be added in the `exports.handler` function before the `handleProductFind()` function:

```
if (event.currentIntent && event.currentIntent.confirmationStatus) {
    let confirmationStatus = event.currentIntent.confirmationStatus;
    if (confirmationStatus == "Denied") {
        console.log('got denied status');
        let message = `Thank you for shopping with us today. Have a nice
```

```
day`
        return Lex.close({message})
    }
    if (confirmationStatus == 'Confirmed'){
        console.log('got confirmed status');
    }
}
```

# Creating the data

Creating the data for this Lambda is not difficult, but there is a lot of data to generate. A record needs to be created for every combination of color, size, and type of item, as well as every pair of trousers needing a short, standard, and long length. Each of these rows needs to be in an array with a key of **stock**.

You can download the completed data file at bit.ly/chatbot-ch6. This file needs to be put into a new bucket called shopping-stock so our Lambda can access it. As in previous chapters, we don't need to change any of the permissions on the bucket or file from their defaults.

# Lambda testing

To test this Lambda, we can create some tests. These tests should test all of the scenarios:

- All of the normal slots filled
- Only the itemNumber slot filled
- Missing a slot value
- A Denied confirmation status
- A Confirmed confirmation status

We need to use four tests to cover all of these scenarios as we can test Confirmed with any of the slot filled scenarios.

In the Lex console, navigate into the productFind Lambda, and at the top of the page click **Configure test events**. The first test event that we can test is missing a slot value. We can actually provide no slot values and we expect that the Lambda will ask us to choose a shirt, jacket, or trousers. This is the input for the first test. Name this test and click **Save**. When you click **Test**, you should get a successful response in the format we expect:

```
{
    "currentIntent": {
        "slots": {
```

```
                    "type": null,
                    "size": null,
                    "colour": null,
                    "length": null,
                    "itemNumber": null
                }
            }
        }
```

Next, we can test for a **Confirmed** confirmation status and all slots filled in one test. Click the dropdown and select **Configure test events** again. This test object now also has `confirmationStatus` on the `currentIntent` object:

```
{
    "currentIntent": {
        "slots": {
            "type": "shirt",
            "size": "medium",
            "colour": "blue",
            "length": null,
            "itemNumber": null
        },
        "confirmationStatus": "Confirmed"
    }
}
```

Similar tests can be created to test `Denied` requests and `itemNumber` requests. The exact code for the tests can be found in the `tests` file in the `productFind` code folder.

## Completing the intent

Now that we have a Lambda to fulfill the intent, we need to go back into Lex and make sure that our intent is triggering that Lambda. As in Chapter 5, *Building Your First Amazon Lex Chatbot*, scroll to the **Fulfillment** section of the intent and select **Lambda fulfillment**. From the drop-down menu, we can choose our new `productFind` Lambda.

Save the intent and we're ready to move on to the next step.

# Add to cart

This intent is a simple intent. If a user says `Yes` to adding the item to the cart, then it adds the item to a cart in Dynamo and asks whether they want to checkout or add another item. If the user says no to adding the item to the cart, then it asks the user whether they want to find another product.

Inside Lex, we need to create a new intent called `addToCart` with a single slot of `itemNumber`. This `itemNumber` slot can be set to have the slot type of **AMAZON.NUMBER** as we've used simple numbers as our item numbers.

As we did in the last Lambda, we need to set this slot to *not be required*. If we required the slot and a user started the intent without one, they would be asked for the item number. Most people won't know items by item number so they wouldn't know what to put. If they enter anything that isn't valid, Lex will re-prompt them for the item number until they guess one or they fail three times. We want to be able to check whether there is an item number and to send them to `productFind` if there isn't.

## Creating the Lambda

To start this Lambda, create another folder in the `Lambda` directory called `addToCart` with an `index.js` file inside. In your folder, we need to run `npm install --save aws-sdk` to make sure that we have access to AWS. We start, as normal, with our default node 8.10 function, and there are two things we need to do at the start of this function: check whether there is a `Denied` confirmation status, and call a `handleAddToCart` function.

If the confirmation status is `denied`, we can ask the user whether they want to find another product, using `Lex.confirmIntent`. We have already programmed our `productFind` Lambda to deal with `confirmIntent` triggers so that should already be working:

```
exports.handler = async (event) => {
    if (event.currentIntent && event.currentIntent.confirmationStatus ===
"Denied"){
        let message = `Would you like to find another product?`;
        let intentName = 'productFind';
        let slots = { type: null, size: null, colour: null, length: null,
itemNumber: null };
        return Lex.confirmIntent({ intentName, slots, message })
    }
    return handleAddToCart(event);
}
```

As we're using the same `Lex.confirmIntent` function as in `productFind`, we need to copy the `LexResponses.js` file into this folder and add this code to the top of this file:

```
const lex = require('./LexResponses');
const Lex = new lex();
```

With the confirmation status dealt with, we can focus on adding the item to the cart. We need to create the `handleAddToCart` function; the first thing that this needs to do is check that we have an `itemNumber`. This check will be very similar to the checks at the start of our `productFind` Lambda, except a missing `itemNumber` will trigger `confirmIntent` on `productFind`:

```
const handleAddToCart = async event => {
    let { slots } = event.currentIntent;
    let { itemNumber } = slots;

    if (!itemNumber) {
        let message = `You need to select a product before adding it to a
cart. Would you like to find another product?`;
        let intentName = 'productFind';
        slots = { type: null, size: null, colour: null, length: null,
itemNumber: null };
        return Lex.confirmIntent({ intentName, slots, message })
    }
}
```

If there is an item number, then we need to add the item to the user's cart. Next, we will be creating a new class, called DB, so that we can make requests, but for now we can assume that these methods exist.

To add an item to the user's cart, we need to check whether the user already has a cart. If they don't, the request will error and we need to create a new cart for them. We are using the same *to* error-catching method that we discussed in Chapter 4, *Connecting Your Alexa Skill to External APIs,* for error-handling.

The `shopping-cart` table will contain four keys:

- ID is a string of the conversation ID
- Items is a list of `itemNumbers`
- name is a name you can give to your cart to save it
- TTL is the *time to live* for the data

The TTL is used so that the record is automatically deleted at a set time. This helps keep your database clean, and is very useful if you have to deal with data protection.

We can try to get a record from the database using `DB.get`, which we will create later in this section. If it returns a value, we can use this as the existing cart. If there isn't a `cartUser`, we will create a default cart. To ensure that the name is unique, we'll use a UUID (universally unique identifier) by setting `name` to `uuidv4()`:

```
let [err, cartUser] = await to(DB.get('ID', event.userId, 'shopping-
cart'));
if (!cartUser) {
    cartUser = { ID: event.userId, Items: [], name: uuidv4(), TTL: 0 }
}
```

To get this working, we need to run `npm install --save uuid` while in out Lambda folder. We then need to include this line at the top of the `index.js` file:

```
const uuidv4 = require('uuid/v4');
```

Now we have a value for `cartUser` for both new and existing carts. To update this cart row, we can use the `spread` operator. This takes an object or array and spreads the values into the new object or array. Any values after the spread can overwrite the values in `spread`:

```
let updatedCart = { ...cartUser, Items: [...cartUser.Items, itemNumber],
TTL: Date.now() + 7 * 24 * 60 * 60 * 1000 };
```

This line of code takes the previous cart, adds a new item number to the `Items` list, and changes the *time to live* to be 7 days from now.

With an updated cart, we need to write it to the table. If there is an error writing to the table, we need to tell the user using `Lex.close`:

```
let [writeErr, res] = await to(DB.write(event.userId, updatedCart,
'shopping-cart'));
if (writeErr) {
    let message = `Unfortunately we've had an error on our system and we
can't add this to your cart.`
    return Lex.close({ message });
}
```

If adding the item to the cart worked, we can ask the user whether they want to add another product, checkout, or save the cart. Unlike when we've asked them whether they want to find another product or add this item to a cart, it isn't a *yes/no* question. They should answer with `I want to checkout`, `I want to save my cart`, or `I want to add another item`, which we will set as example utterances for the `checkout`, `saveCart`, and `productFind` intents.

Because we are trying to find out which intent the user wants to use, we can respond to Lex with an `elicitIntent` response:

```
let message = `Would you like to checkout, add another item to your cart or
save your cart for later?`;
return Lex.elicitIntent({ message });
```

# DynamoDB

As we said earlier, we are going to use DynamoDB to store the cart information. We are going to have two Dynamo tables, one for current carts and one for placed orders. To create these, we need to go onto the AWS console and navigate to the `DynamoDB` service:

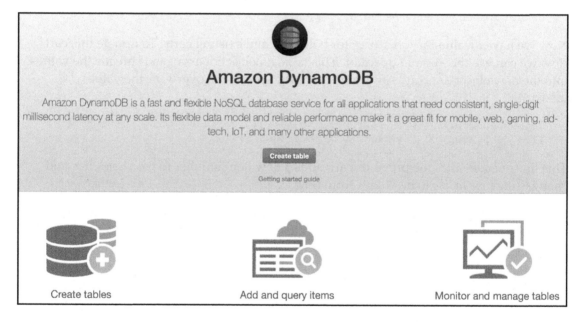

DynamoDB console page

Click **Create table** to start creating a new table. We are asked to name our table and select a primary key. We're going to call our first table `shopping-cart` and set the **Primary key** to `ID`. The primary key is the value that we will be able to use to look up records, and it is best practice to use `ID` as the name of the **Primary key**:

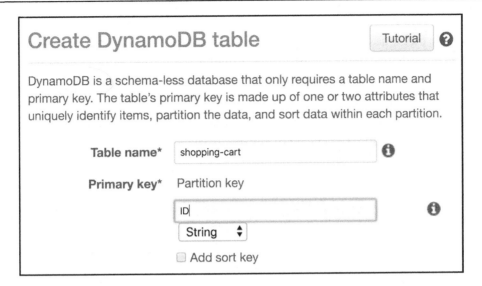

Table creation

When we click the **Create** button, we will be taken to the main DynamoDB console page. There is a lot of information available on this page, but we only need to see that we have our `shopping-cart` table in the table list. When you have just created the table, it may have a loading indicator next to it as the creation process finishes.

With our table created, we need to write some code that allows us to work with it. Because we will be working with Dynamo in multiple intents and Lambdas, it is good practice to create reusable code. For this, we will create a `DB` class that provides methods to get, write, update, and deletes record from the database. Create a new file called `DB.js` in our `addToCart` folder, and inside we're going to create a new class:

```
module.exports = class DB {};
```

To allow us to access the Dynamo tables, AWS provides us with a DynamoDB document client. To create `documentClient`, we need to pass in a configuration object containing the region. This code can go at the top of our `DB` file.

Make sure to change your region to the region that your tables are located in. This should be either `eu-west-1` or `us-east-1`. If you are not sure, go to your AWS console and check your location setting. **Ireland** is `eu-west-1` and **US East (N. Virginia)** is `us-east-1`:

```
const AWS = require('aws-sdk');
let documentClient = new AWS.DynamoDB.DocumentClient({
    'region': 'eu-west-1'
});
```

Now that we've created our `documentClient` variable, we can move back into our class and create our methods. The first method that we are going to make is `write`. We need three things to write to a table: the row ID, the data that we want to write, and the table name.

To improve the usability of this class, we're going to return a `Promise`. Inside this `Promise`, we first need to check the `ID`, `data`, and `table`. If any of them are missing, or if `ID` or `table` aren't strings, we need to throw an error:

```
write(ID, data, table) {
    return new Promise((resolve, reject) => {
        if (!ID) throw 'An ID is needed';
        if (typeof ID !== 'string') throw `the id must be a string and not
${ID}`
        if (!data) throw "data is needed";
        if (!table) throw 'table name is needed';
        if (typeof table !== 'string') throw `the table must be a string
and not ${table}`;
    })
}
```

If `ID`, `data`, and `table` are all correct, we can write our data to the table. To write to a table, we need to pass the request into a specific format. The `Item` needs to be all of the data with an added `ID` field with a value of the row ID that we pass in:

```
let params = {
    TableName: table,
    Item: { ...data, ID: ID }
};
```

This `params` object can then be passed into the `documentClient.put()` method, which also takes a `callback` function. We `console.log` out the error or data from the response before resolving the data or rejecting the error:

```
documentClient.put(params, function(err, result) {
    if (err) {
        console.log("Err in writeForCall writing messages to dynamo:",
err);
        console.log(params);
        return reject(err);
    }
    console.log('wrote data to table ', table)
    return resolve({ ...result.Attributes, ...params.Item });
});
```

As we are creating this class, we are going to create the `get`, `update`, and `delete` methods as well.

`get` is very similar to `write`, taking just a `key`, `value`, and `table`. Instead of passing in the items that we want to write, we pass in the key that we want to match. This `key-value` pair needs to be set inside `params`:

```
get(key, value, table) {
    if (!table) throw 'table needed';
    if (typeof key !== 'string') throw `key was not string and was
${JSON.stringify(key)} on table ${table}`;
    if (typeof value !== 'string') throw `value was not string and was
${JSON.stringify(value)} on table ${table}`;
    return new Promise((resolve, reject) => {
        let params = {
            TableName: table,
            Key: { [key]: value }
        };
        documentClient.get(params, function(err, data) {
            if (err) {
                console.log(`There was an error fetching the data for
${key} ${value} on table ${table}`, err);
                return reject(err);
            }
            //TODO check only one Item.
            return resolve(data.Item);
        });
    });
}
```

`get` works as you would expect for getting items based on the primary index, but what if we want to get items by a second value? We can't use `documentClient.get()`, so we need to create a new function called `getDifferent`. This function uses `documentClient.query()` instead of `documentClient.get()`:

```
getDifferent(key, value, table) {
    if (!table) throw 'table needed';
    if (typeof key !== 'string') throw `key was not string and was
${JSON.stringify(key)} on table ${table}`;
    if (typeof value !== 'string') throw `value was not string and was
${JSON.stringify(value)} on table ${table}`;
    if (!table) 'table needs to be users, sessions, or routes.'
    return new Promise((resolve, reject) => {
        var params = {
            TableName : table,
            IndexName : `${key}-index`,
            KeyConditionExpression : `${key} = :value`,
```

```
                    ExpressionAttributeValues : {
                        ':value' : value
                    }
            };

            documentClient.query(params, function(err, data) {
                if (err) {
                    console.error("Unable to read item. Error JSON:",
    JSON.stringify(err));
                    reject(err);
                } else {
                    console.log("GetItem succeeded:",
    JSON.stringify(data.Items));
                    resolve(data.Items);
                }
            });
        })
    }
```

delete is almost identical to get, with the main difference being that we call
documentClient.delete:

```
delete(ID, table) {
    if (!table) throw 'table needed';
    if (typeof ID !== 'string') throw `ID was not string and was
${JSON.stringify(ID)} on table ${table}`;
    console.log("dynamo deleting record ID", ID, 'from table ', table);
    let params = {
        TableName: table,
        Key: { 'ID': ID  }
    };

    return new Promise((resolve, reject) => {
        documentClient.delete(params, function(err, data) {
            if (err) {
                reject(err);
            } else {
                resolve(data);
            }
        });
    });
}
```

The last method that we need to create is `update`. This is a very simple method as it just uses the other methods to do most of the work. It gets the data for the `ID` and then writes it back with the new key and value added on or changed:

```
async update(ID, table, key, value) {
    let data = await this.get(ID, table);
    return this.write(ID, { ...data, [key]: value }, table);
}
```

Now that we've completed the `DB` class, we need to import it into our Lambda and create a new instance. At the top of our `index.js` file in the `addToCart` folder, we can add these lines:

```
const db = require('./DB');
const DB = new db();
```

Our Lambdas have to deal with Dynamo as well as S3; we need to give these Lambdas the permissions they need to do this.

Open up the AWS console and navigate to AIM. Under **Roles** in the menu on the left, find the role that we created back in Chapter 2, *Getting Started with AWS and Amazon CLI*. We're going to add Dynamo permissions to this role.

# Adding Dynamo permissions

Now that our Lambdas are working with Dynamo and S3, we need to update our permissions the role that we use to build our Lambdas. Navigate to the IAM service and select the **lambdaBasic** role that we created in Chapter 2, *Getting Started with AWS and Amazon CLI*. Click **Attach policy** and search for Dynamo.

We need to add **AmazonDynamoDBFullAccess**. This gives the Lambda permissions to read and write to Dynamo:

Adding DynamoDB policies

# Testing

Before we run any testing, we need to build and deploy our Lambda. Using the build script we created in Chapter 2, *Getting Started with AWS and Amazon CLI*, we can run `./build.sh addToCart` to build and deploy our new Lambda.

With this complete, we can navigate to our Lambda console and select our new `addToCart` Lambda. Next to **Test**, we can click **Configure test events**.

There are things that we need to test for this Lambda:

- A `Denied` confirmation status
- A `Confirmed` confirmation status
- A trigger without an `itemNumber`
- Adding an item to a new cart
- Adding an item to an existing cart

A `Denied` trigger is the easiest to test. You should get a response asking `Would you like to find another product?`:

```
{ "currentIntent": { "confirmationStatus": "Denied" } }
```

We can test a `Confirmed` confirmation status and a trigger without an `itemNumber` in one test. We should get through to the `handleAddToCart` function, and then get a response telling us we need to select a product and asking whether we want to find one:

```
{
    "currentIntent": {
        "confirmationStatus": "Confirmed",
        "slots": {
            "itemNumber": null
        }
    }
}
```

The test for adding an item to a new cart and to an existing cart will be the same; you just have to run the test twice. The first time, there won't be any existing order. The second time, there will be. You need to change the `ID` value every time you want to test a new cart:

```
{
    "currentIntent": {
        "slots": {
            "itemNumber": 1034
        }
    },
    "userId": "123-sdf-654-hjk2"
}
```

Both times, you should get a response asking `Would you like to checkout or add another item to your basket?`.

The last thing we need to do is to add this tested Lambda as the handler for the intent. Navigate to the Lex chatbot and to the `addToCart` intent. In the **Fulfillment** section of the page, we can change the fulfillment to **Lambda fulfillment** and select our new `addToCart` Lambda to fulfill it.

# Checkout

When a user wants to checkout, we are going to do a simplified checkout process. We are just going to ask them for a mailing address and tell them we'll collect payment on delivery. Behind the scenes, we're going to take their cart and move it into a new `shopping-orders` table.

To start, we need to create a new intent in Lex called `checkout`. We can add utterances such as `I want to checkout`, `can I checkout please`, and just `checkout`. You can add more utterances that you expect a user might reply to, such as `Would you like to checkout or add another item to your basket?`.

We can access their cart using the *userId* on the event so the only other information we need is their `deliveryAddress` – so we need to add that as a slot. The slot type for this slot can be set to **AMAZON.PostalAddress** and we can add a prompt of `What address do you want your products delivered to?`. We can set this slot to be required so that whenever this intent is triggered. This means that we should already have the delivery address when the fulfillment Lambda gets triggered:

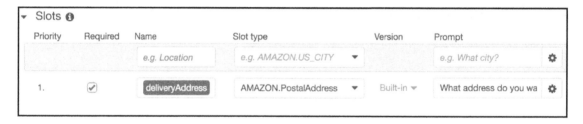

Checkout slot

# Creating the Lambda

With the intent set up, we can create the Lambda. Create a new folder called `checkout` and add an `index.js` file. In your folder, we need to run `npm install --save aws-sdk`. We are going to start with the node 8.10 handler with the `confirmationStatus` check for a denied status. We may want to trigger this intent with `confirmIntent` in the future:

```
exports.handler = async (event) => {
    if (event.currentIntent && event.currentIntent.confirmationStatus ===
"Denied") {
        let message = `Would you like to find another product?`;
        let intentName = 'productFind';
        slots = { type: null, size: null, colour: null, length: null,
```

```
itemNumber: null };
        return Lex.confirmIntent({ intentName, slots, message })
    }
    return handleCheckout(event);
}
```

We have already used `Lex` again, so we need to copy our `LexResponse.js` file into this folder and use our setup code at the top of the file:

```
const lex = require('./LexResponses');
const Lex = new lex();
```

Now we can get into the bulk of this Lambda with our `handleCheckout` function. We are first going to check that we have a value in the `deliveryAddress` slot. If we don't, then we'll ask them for it using `elicitSlot`:

```
const handleCheckout = async event => {
    let { slots } = event.currentIntent;
    let { deliveryAddress } = slots;

    if (!deliveryAddress) {
        let message = `What address would you like this order delivered
to?`;
        let intentName = 'checkout';
        slots = { deliveryAddress: null };
        let slotToElicit = 'deliveryAddress';
        return Lex.elicitSlot({message, intentName, slots, slotToElicit});
    }
}
```

Once we know that we have a delivery address, we can turn their cart into an order. To do this, we'll get their cart and then put that into a `shopping-orders` table with their delivery address and date of order.

Before we can create the code, we need to set up a new table in DynamoDB. Navigate to the Dynamo console in AWS and click **Create table**. Name our new table `shopping-orders` and give it a primary key of `ID`.

Back in our Lambda code, we can now create the logic to place the order. First we need to get the cart, and then delete that cart. If we get an error, then we need to tell the user and ask whether there is anything else we can help them with:

```
let [cartErr, cart] = await to(DB.get("ID", event.userId, 'shopping-
cart'));
if (!cart){
    console.log('no cart');
    let message = `We couldn't find your cart. Is there anything else I can
```

```
help you with`;
    return Lex.elicitIntent({ message });
}
```

If we successfully got a cart back, we can delete the cart, create a new `orders` object, and write that to our `shopping-orders` table. We delete the cart because we don't expect to place an order and still have all of the items in your cart:

```
let order = { Items: cart.Items, address: deliveryAddress, date: Date.now()
};
let ID = uuidv4();
```

We generate a random ID by using `uuidv4()` again. This means that we also need to run `npm install --save uuid` and include `const uuidv4 = require('uuid/v4');` at the top of this file.

We will use a `try/catch` for this as it allows us to make both of the requests and handle any errors in a single handler. If an error is thrown, it is likely that our code is wrong so we don't want to make the user go through that again. Therefore, we'll tell them there was an error and their order can't be placed:

```
try {
    await to(DB.write(ID, order, 'shopping-orders'));
    await to(DB.delete(event.userId, 'shopping-cart'));
} catch (err) {
    console.log('error deleting the cart or writing the order', cartErr)
    let message = `I'm sorry, there was a system error so your order hasn't
been placed.`;
    return Lex.close({ message });
}
```

If there wasn't an error, we can tell the user that their order was placed:

```
let message = `Thank you. Your order has been placed and will be delivered
in 3-5 working days`;
return Lex.close({ message });
```

With all paths of the intent completed, we can use our build script to build and deploy our Lambda before testing. Navigate into your `Lambdas` folder and run the following code:

```
./build.sh checkout
```

# Testing

With this Lambda, there are a few scenarios to test:

- Confirmed intent
- Denied intent
- No delivery address
- The user doesn't have a cart to checkout
- The user has a cart

A `Denied` intent should ask us whether we want to find a new product:

```
{ "currentIntent": { "confirmationStatus": "Denied" } }
```

The `Confirmed` intent and no delivery address can be tested together. We expect the status to have no effect on the process, and the response to ask us for our delivery address:

```
{
    "currentIntent": {
        "confirmationStatus": "Confirmed",
        "slots": { "deliveryAddress": null}
    }
}
```

To test a user without a cart, we can call the Lambda with a `userId` that would never have an order. We can choose a normal word as this will never be used as a `userID` in Lex:

```
{
  "currentIntent": {
  "confirmationStatus": "None",
  "slots": { "deliveryAddress": "123 imaginary street, fake town,
madeupsville"}
  },
  "userId": "fakeUser"
}
```

From this test, we should be told `We couldn't find your cart.` and then asked whether we want to find a product.

The last scenario is a successful order placement. This will need a little more work as we need to find a valid cart. To do this, we can go onto AWS and navigate to Dynamo. Select the `shopping-orders` table and then we can click the **Items** tab. This allows us to look directly at the items in our table so we can find a valid cart ID. Copy any of the IDs, and paste it as the value in this next test case:

```
{
    "currentIntent": {
        "confirmationStatus": "None",
        "slots": { "deliveryAddress": "123 imaginary street, fake town,
madeupsville"}
    },
    "userId": ## paste your ID here
}
```

From this, we expect to get a response telling us that we have successfully placed an order. We can also check in our `shopping-orders` table that we have a new row. When running this test, we need to use a valid cart ID. Unfortunately, when we create an order, we delete the old cart, meaning that the ID is no longer valid so we need to get a new ID for every test.

As with all of the Lambdas and intents so far, the last thing we need to do is add this tested Lambda as the handler for the intent. Navigate to the Lex chatbot and then to the **checkout** intent. In the **Fulfillment** section of the page, we can change the fulfillment to **Lambda fulfillment** and select our new **checkout** Lambda to fulfill it.

# Saving our cart

So far, we have created the flow for the perfect conversation, one where the user finds one or more products, adds them to their cart, and checks out straight away. This is good, but a lot of people will add things to their cart, leave, and then come back to checkout.

We need to create an intent that lets the user save their cart and come back to it later to checkout. Most shopping websites will have a login system or use web caching to save a cart to a user, but we're going to save a cart by a *unique name*.

In our Lex console for this chatbot, we can add a new `saveCart` intent. At the end of the `addToCart` intent, we ask the user whether they want to `add another product`, `save your cart`, or `checkout`. We need to handle the utterances that the user might say to save their cart. Add utterances such as `save my cart` and `I want to save my cart for later`.

The `cart` and `basket` words are very similar in meaning, so add some utterances with each of them:

saveCart sample utterances

We only need one slot for this intent. Add a slot of `cartName` with a slot type of **AMAZON.Musician** and a prompt of `What name would you like to save your cart as?`. Using a slot type of **Musician** might seem strange, but this slot type allows any value to be accepted, thereby allowing users to name their basket whatever they want. We can set the `cartName` slot to be required, as we'll always need a name to save the cart as.

## Creating the Lambda

Create a new folder in the `Lambdas` folder, called `saveCart`, with an `index.js` file in it. In that `index.js` file, we're going to start, as normal, with the node 8.10 async handler. We know that we are going to be using Lex responses and accessing dynamo, so we add those files and require them into our `index.js`:

```
const lex = require('./LexResponses');
const Lex = new lex();
const db = require('./DB');
const DB = new db();

exports.handler = async (event) => {
    return handleSaveCart(event);
}
```

As we're going to be using Dynamo, we need to make sure to install `aws-sdk` by running `npm install --save aws-sdk`.

With this intent, we are never going to be doing `confirmIntent` on it, so we don't need to handle any confirmation status. This means the only function in our handler is a `handleSaveCart(event)` function.

Inside the `handleSaveCart` function, we need to get `userID` and `slots` from the event. We can then get `cartName` from the slots:

```
const handleSaveCart = async event => {
    let { slots } = event.currentIntent;
    let { cartName } = slots;
}
```

We first need to check that there is a `cartName` as there always needs to be. This should never be called since the `cartName` slot is required, but it is always safer to put it in:

```
if (!cartName) {
    let message = `You need to save your cart with a name. What do you want
to call it?`;
    let intentName = 'saveCart';
    slots = { cartName: null };
    let slotToElicit = 'cartName';
    return Lex.elicitSlot({ intentName, slotToElicit, slots, message });
}
```

Now that we have a valid cart name, we first need to see whether the user has a cart to checkout. If they don't, then we ask them whether they want to add an item to their cart:

```
let [err, cart] = await to(DB.get('ID', event.userId, 'shopping-cart'));
if (err || !cart || !cart.Items) {
    let message = `You don't have a cart. Would you like to find a
product?`;
    let intentName = 'productFind';
    slots = { type: null, size: null, colour: null, length: null,
itemNumber: null };
    return Lex.confirmIntent({ intentName, slots, message });
}
```

Next, we can check whether there is already a cart with that name. To do this, we can try getting the cart with that name. If we can't find a cart with that name it means that we won't over-ride another cart when we save. If we do find a cart with that name, then we need to ask the user for a new cart name:

```
let [getCartErr, getCarts] = await to(DB.getDifferent('cartName', cartName,
'shopping-cart'));
```

```
if (!getCarts || !getCarts[0] ) {
    // No cart with that name so we can save the current cart to this name
    return addNameToCart(cart, cartName);
}
let message = `Unfortunately you can't use that name. Please choose another
name.`;
let intentName = 'saveCart';
let slotToElicit = 'cartName';
slots = { cartName: null };
return Lex.elicitSlot({ intentName, slots, slotToElicit, message });
```

To save their cart using that cart name, we return a function to add the name to the cart. This function starts by setting the cart name as the passed-in slot value:

```
const addNameToCart = async (cart, cartName) => {
    cart.cartName = cartName;
}
```

Now we can carry on this function by writing the cart back to the table. If there is an error, we tell the user we can't save their cart, otherwise we tell them it's been saved and how to access it next time:

```
let [err, res] = await to(DB.write(cart.ID, cart, 'shopping-cart'));
if (err) {
    console.log('err writing cart with name', err);
    let message = `Unfortunately we cant save your cart`;
    return Lex.close({ message });
}
let message = `Your cart has been saved. Type "find my cart" next time and
enter "${cartName}" to get this cart.`;
return Lex.close({ message });
```

As always, make sure to run the build script to deploy your Lambda.

# Dynamo changes

In this Lambda, we did `DB.get` using the `cartName` instead of the `ID`. To get this working, we need to index our table by `cartName`. Creating an index for a key allow us to search by the values. This is also why we set the default name for a cart to `uuidv4()`. Because we can search by the name, it needs to be unique.

Navigate to the Dynamo service in AWS and select the `shopping-cart` table. Across the top of this section is a row of tabs, and we're going to choose **Indexes** and click **Create index**. This will open a popup where we need to enter the key we want to index, in this case, `cartName`. Click **Create index** and the index will start to be created:

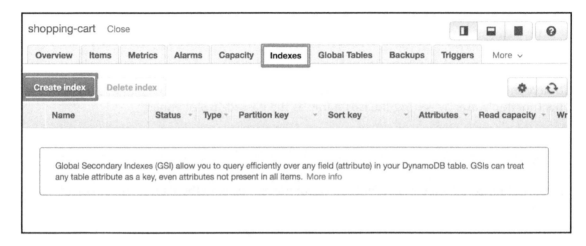

Secondary index

When this finishes the creation process, we will be able to do `getDifferent` requests on this table by `cartName`.

# Testing

Testing our `saveCart` intent requires only dealing with four scenarios: *no cart name, no cart to save, cart name already taken,* and *saving a cart.*

Testing when there is no cart name is very simple. We expect this to ask us to give a name for our cart:

```
{
    "currentIntent": {
        "slots": {
            "cartName": null
        }
    }
}
```

To test saving when we don't have a cart, we can use a nonsense `userId` as there is no chance that there will be a cart for them. We need to pass in a valid `cartName` now so that we pass the first check:

```
{
    "currentIntent": {
        "slots": {
            "cartName": "personalShopping"
        }
    },
    "userId": "asdasdasdasdasd"
}
```

We are going to have to test the last two in a different order. We first test a successful saving of a cart. To do this, we need a `userId` with a cart. We can find that by going into our Dynamo console and looking at the **Items** tab on our `shopping-cart` table. Choose any of the IDs that are there and copy it into the `userId` value in the test object.

We expect that this will be successful and we'll be told how to get our cart next time:

```
{
    "currentIntent": {
        "slots": {
            "cartName": "testCartSave"
        }
    },
    "userId": ## valid userId
}
```

Now that we have saved a cart, we can try saving a different cart with the same name. We have to find a new `ID` for this test but leave the rest of the request the same.

This time, we should be told that we can't use that cart name and to try a different one:

```
{
    "currentIntent": {
        "slots": {
            "cartName": "testCartSave"
        }
    },
    "userId": ## another valid userId
}
```

With all of the tests responding as we expected, go back into the Lex console for this bot and change the fulfillment of the *saveCart* intent to the `saveCart` Lambda.

# Retrieving a saved cart

Now that the user can save their cart, we need to give them a way to get the cart that they saved. We can then change the cart so that it matches their `userId`, and then they can continue to add more items or checkout.

Create a new `getSavedCart` intent in Lex, and we're only going to be asking for the `cartName` of the cart they saved. As we did in the `saveCart` intent, we can set the `cartName` slot type to **AMAZON.Musician** to allow any values through. We can also set this slot to be required and have a prompt of `"What was the name you saved your cart to?"`.

Unlike with the other intents so far, we can allow the user to enter the `cartName` as part of the utterance. This is done by including the slot name in the utterance with curly brackets around it. This can be used for utterances such as `"I want to get cart { cartName }"`.

As well as utterances that include the `cartName`, we will still have normal utterances such as `"I want to get my saved cart"` or `"get my cart"`. This utterance will get Lex to prompt the user for the `cartName` using the prompt we provided:

Utterances for getSavedCart

# Creating the Lambda

We start by creating a `getSavedCart` folder in our `Lambdas` directory, and inside we're going to have an `index.js` file and copy our `DB.js` and `LexResponses.js` files from our previous Lambdas. Our `index.js` file will start as normal, with us importing and initiating our `DB` and `Lex` classes and using the node 8.10 handler. We need to make sure to run `npm install --save aws-sdk` in our folder as well. We'll never do a confirmed intent on this intent, so we only need to handle a `getSavedCart` event:

```
const lex = require('./LexResponses');
const Lex = new lex();
const db = require('./DB');
const DB = new db();

exports.handler = async (event) => {
    return handleGetSavedCart(event);
}
```

The first thing we need to do in our Lambda is to get our `userId`, `slots`, and our `cartName` slot. We can then check that we have a `cartName` or ask the user for it if we don't:

```
const handleGetSavedCart = event => {
    let { userId, currentIntent: { slots } } = event;
    let { cartName } = slots;

    if (!cartName) {
        let message = `What name did you save your cart as?`;
        let intentName = 'getSavedCart';
        let slotToElicit = 'cartName';
        let slots = { cartName: null };
        return Lex.elicitSlot({ intentName, slots, slotToElicit, message
});
    }
}
```

Now that we know we have a `cartName`, we can try to get the cart with that name. If we can't get a cart with that name, then we need to ask whether they want to try another name or start a new cart. This will have to be an `elicitIntent` as they could go with either of two intents:

```
let [err, carts] = await to(DB.getDifferent('cartName', cartName,
'shopping-cart'));
if (err || !carts || !carts[0]) {
```

```
        let message = `We couldn't find a cart with that name. Would you
    like to try another name or start a new cart?`;
        return Lex.elicitIntent({message});
    }
```

To get this `elicitIntent` to work, we need to also add the utterance of `try another name` to `getSavedCart`, and `start a new cart` to the `productFind` intent.

`DB.getDifferent` gets an array of matching carts, which is why we're looking for `carts[0]`. We also need to extract our cart by adding this line after our error-handler:

```
    let cart = carts[0];
```

If we found a cart for that `cartName`, then we need to do two things. We need to create a cart with those items on their current `userId`, and then we need to delete the old cart. If we don't delete the old cart, there will be two carts with the same name.

We can create the new cart by changing the ID and updating the TTL on the old cart. We also need to store the ID of the old cart so we can delete it too:

```
    let cart = carts[0];
    let oldCartID = cart.ID;
    let newCart = { ...cart, ID: userId, TTL: Date.now() + 7 * 24 * 60 * 60 *
    1000 };
```

When we create the new cart and delete the old one, we can wrap them both in `try/catch` and handle any errors in the same way. If there are any errors, then we need to tell the user that we couldn't recover their cart and ask whether they want to start a new cart. This can be a `confirmIntent` on the `productFind` intent, which will start them at the beginning of the flow again.

If there's no error, then we can tell them that we have got their cart and ask whether they want to checkout or get another item:

```
    try {
        await DB.write(userId, newCart, 'shopping-cart');
        await DB.delete(oldCartID, 'shopping-cart');
    } catch (createErr) {
        let message = `Unfortunately we couldn't recover your cart. Would you
    like to create a new cart?`;
        let intentName = 'productFind';
        let slots = { type: null, size: null, colour: null, length: null,
    itemNumber: null };
        return Lex.confirmIntent({ intentName, slots, message });
    }
```

```
let message = `We have got your cart for you. Would you like to checkout or
add another product?`;
return Lex.elicitIntent({ message });
```

That is the end of this Lambda, so now we can build and deploy using our script and move
on to testing it.

# Testing

To test this, we need to test three things:

- No `cartName`
- A non-existent `cartName`
- Successfully getting their cart

Testing no cart name is very simple. We expect to get a response asking for the cart name:

```
{
    "currentIntent": {
        "slots": {
            "cartName": null
        }
    }
}
```

To test a non-existent cart name, we need to use a name that someone isn't going to use. We
expect the response to say that a cart with that name couldn't be found:

```
{
    "currentIntent": {
        "slots": {
            "cartName": "nonsense"
        }
    }
}
```

The last test requires us to look in the Dynamo tables again. This time, we are looking for
an order with a valid name. If we completed the tests for `saveCart`, we should have a cart
called `testCartSave`. This request should get a response saying that the cart has been
found and asking whether they want to checkout or find another product:

```
{
    "currentIntent": {
        "slots": {
```

```
                "cartName": "testCartSave"
            }
        }
    }
```

Once all of these tests pass, we can add this Lambda as the fulfillment method for our getSavedCart intent.

# What's in my cart?

This is the last intent we are going to make in this chapter. When a user asks what they have in their cart, we are going to give them a summary. This involves getting their cart and matching their item numbers up with the data in S3.

When we create this intent in Lex, we don't need any slots—the only information we need is their userId. The utterances will be questions about what is in their cart, such as what is in my cart and how much have I got in my basket.

## Creating the Lambda

We create a new folder called whatsInMyCart in our Lambda directory with an index.js file, as well as copying DB.js and LexResponses.js into this folder.

This function is going to need to access Dynamo to access the baskets and S3 to get the product data. We start the index.js file by requiring in DB.js, LexResponses.js, and aws-sdk, and then creating new DB, Lex, and S3 class instances. We don't have any confirmations on this intent, so we can just return a handleWhatsInMyCart function:

```
const lex = require('./LexResponses');
const Lex = new lex();
const db = require('./DB');
const DB = new db();
const AWS = require('aws-sdk');
const s3 = new AWS.S3();

exports.handler = async (event) => {
    return handleWhatsInMyCart(event);
}
```

When a user triggers this intent, the first thing we need to do is get their cart. If they don't have a cart, then we need to remind them that they can recover a saved cart or add new items to their existing cart:

```
const handleWhatsInMyCart = async event => {
    let [err, cart] = await to(DB.get('ID', event.userId, 'shopping-
cart'));
    if (err || !cart || cart.Items.length == 0) {
        let message = `You don't appear to have a cart. If you have saved a
cart then you can recover it by typing "Get my cart", or you can say "I
want to buy something"`;
        return Lex.elicitIntent({ message });
    }
}
```

If they do have a cart, then we can reformat the items into their cart into a more manageable format. The way that items are added to the cart, multiples of the same item are just separate items in the array. We can use some array logic to convert this into an object with item numbers as keys, which point to objects containing the quantity. This code goes through each item, and if we have already added that item to the `items` object, it adds 1 to the quantity. If this is the first unit of this item, then it sets the quantity to 1:

```
let items = {};
cart.Items.map(item => {
    items[item] = (items[item] && items[item].quantity) ? { quantity:
items[item].quantity + 1 } : { quantity: 1 };
});
```

With our object of items, we need to map this to item descriptions. For this, we need the data from S3. We can copy the same `getStock()` function that we used in `productFind` into this Lambda. If there is an error or we don't get back a list of products, we need to tell the user that we have had a problem:

```
const [s3Err, products] = await to(getStock());
if (s3Err || !products) {
    let message = `Unfortunately our system has had an error.`;
    Lex.close({ message });
}
```

We have our object of items and all of our products. We can use this to expand the data in our `items` object. To do this, we can map over each of the `products` and, if the `itemNumber` is in our `items` object, we add those details to that item's data:

```
products.forEach(product => {
    if (items[product.itemNumber]){
        items[product.itemNumber] = { ...product,
...items[product.itemNumber]};
    }
});
```

We have an object that contains all the data we need. We can map over this and create a string describing the item and quantity. We can use the `Object.values()` method, which turns an object into an array that contains the values. Here is an example:

```
let data = {
    name: { firstName: 'Tom', lastName: 'Jones' },
    age: 25,
    height: '178 cm'
};

console.log(Object.values(data));
// [ { firstName: 'Tom', lastName: 'Jones' }, 25 , '178cm' ]
```

We can use this to get the data for each of the items to create `itemStrings`, such as `2 blue jackets` or `1 long, black pair of trousers`. We can use the `units()` function that we created in `productFind` to deal with the units and with trousers:

```
let itemStrings = Object.values(items).map(item => {
    let { type, size, colour, length, quantity } = item;
    return `${quantity} ${size}, ${length ? `${length}, ` : ''}${colour}
${units(type, quantity)}`;
});
```

We can now join this array of item strings together into a one-cart summary. If there is one item, we can just say that item. Two items mean we need to add and between them, and we need to separate three or more items with commas:

```
let message = `You have ${itemStrings.slice(0,-1).join(',
')}${itemStrings.length > 1 ? ` and ` : ""}${itemStrings.pop()} in your
cart. Would you like to checkout, save your cart or add another item?`;
```

With our message created, all we have left to do is to return our `Lex` response, which will be an `elicitIntent` response:

```
return Lex.elicitIntent({ message });
```

With the Lambda completed, we need to build and deploy it, and move on to testing.

## Testing

There are only two situations to test for in this Lambda:

- No cart
- Successful cart lookup

To test for no cart, we can provide a non-existent `userId`. We should get a response telling us that our cart can't be found:

```
{
    "userId": "nonsense"
}
```

To test a successful cart lookup, we need to go into our Dynamo table and find a cart with items in it. We should get a nicely formatted sentence describing the items in the cart and be asked whether we want to checkout, save, or add another item:

```
{
    "userId": ## valid userID
}
```

With the testing complete, we can go into the Lex bot and change the fulfilment for the `whatsInMyCart` intent to our `whatsInMyCart` Lambda.

## Testing the whole bot

Now that we have created all of the Lambdas and tested that they all work, we can put it all together and build our chatbot. On the Lex console for this chatbot, go through each of the intents and make sure that they are all being fulfilled using the correct Lambda, and then we can click **Build** at the top of the page.

Once it has finished building, we can start testing it out. We can start with finding a product. Typing I want to buy a shirt starts the productFind intent flow, and we can find the stock levels of the found item:

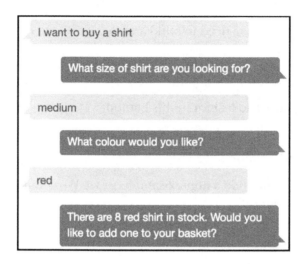

Testing productFind

When we get shown a product, we should also be asked whether we want to add this to our cart. No matter our answer, we should then be asked whether we want to **checkout, add another item,** or **save our cart**. We need to try each of these methods, starting with adding another item:

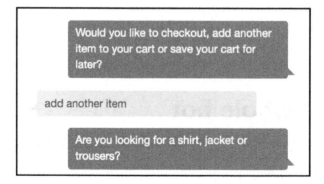

Adding another item to the cart

As expected, we are sent to the start of the `productFind` flow. Having gone through that flow but not added a new item to our cart, we can now test saving our cart. When we get to the end of a product find, we can say that we want to save our cart. When we provide a cart name, we are told that our cart has been saved:

Testing saveCart

To test recovering a cart, we can clear the chat in Lex and ask to `get my saved cart`. We should be asked to enter our cart name and, if found, it will be recovered for us:

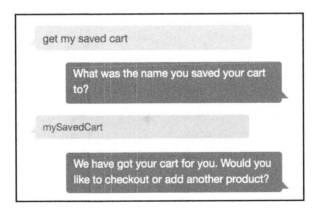

Testing getSavedCart

Now that we've got our saved cart back, we might want to check what we put in it. All we need to say is `what is in my cart` and we should get a summary of our products. As we only added the first product, we should have just one item:

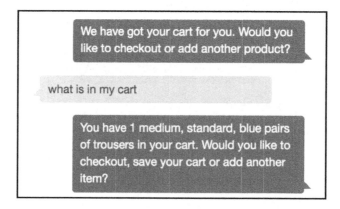

Testing whatsInMyCart

The last thing to test is checking out. With at least one item in our basket, we can ask to checkout. We should be asked for an address and then be told that our order has been placed:

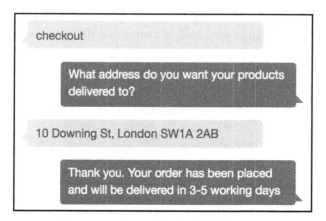

Testing checkout

With all of that tested, we have completed our shopping chatbot. If you've had any problems with these tests, go back and make sure that all of your code is correct and that Lex has been set up correctly. If you are having further issues, there is a set of debugging tips at the end of this book.

# Summary

This chapter has covered a lot. We started by designing a complex chatbot flow with multiple sub-flows. We then built these flows into a set of intents, which allow a user to go through the full process, or to do part of the process and return later. This meant we need to trigger intents directly from other intents, pre-populating some of the slots and using *confirmation intents* to change from one intent to another. We've also learned how to use DynamoDB tables to store and retrieve data about the progress of the users.

# Questions

1. What is the main difference between a complex flow and a simple flow?
2. How can we make complex flow diagrams easier to understand?
3. What are the five types of Lex fulfillment?
4. What is the name of the part of the AWS SDK that we can use to access DynamoDB tables?

# Further reading

If you want to learn more about the different ways to interact with Dynamo, I would recommend looking through the DocumentClient documentation. You can learn how to implement scans, queries, and batch processing. You can read that documentation at `https://docs.aws.amazon.com/AWSJavaScriptSDK/latest/AWS/DynamoDB/DocumentClient.html`.

# 7
# Publishing Your Chatbot to Facebook, Slack, Twilio, and HTTP

We've learned how to build a range of chatbots using Amazon Lex, but currently, no one else can access them. In this chapter, we're going to learn how we can deploy our chatbots onto Facebook, Slack, and Twilio. We'll also learn how to integrate Lex with our own frontend and also create an HTTP endpoint, allowing more flexible integrations.

The following topics will be covered in this chapter:

- Deploying Lex chatbots to Facebook Messenger, Slack, and Twilio
- Creating an HTTP endpoint to allow more flexible integrations
- Building a frontend for our chatbot

## Technical requirements

In this chapter, we will be creating a Lambda function to power our HTTP endpoint, and we'll be creating and deploying it using the local development setup that we created in Chapter 2, *Getting Started with AWS and Amazon CLI*.

We'll also be using Facebook and Slack, so you need to have an account. If you don't already, you can create accounts for free.

All of the code and data required for this chapter can be found at `bit.ly/chatbot-ch7`.

# Integrations

Having built a chatbot, you want users to be able to find it and use it. A lot of your users will already have Facebook or Slack, and they'll definitely have a mobile number. Being able to use our chatbots through these existing communication methods makes it a lot easier and more natural for our users.

To allow chatbots onto their systems, Facebook, Slack, and Twilio have created integration methods. This allows messages that are sent through each of those platforms to reach our chatbot, making our chatbot appear to be part of the system.

Amazon Lex makes it very easy for us to integrate with Facebook, Slack, Twilio, and Kik, hiding a lot of complex data formatting behind the scenes. To access the integrations that Lex has, click on the **Channels** tab, and you'll have the choice to configure Facebook, Kik, Slack, or Twilio SMS.

# Facebook Messenger

The Facebook Messenger had 1.3 billion monthly users as of April 2018, and that number has been growing month on month. This is a huge user base that we can tap into.

As well as the massive user base, there's another great feature for chatbot developers. When you create a Facebook page for a company, organization, or anything else, it has a Messenger account. This is so that users can message the company, but this means that every company on Facebook could benefit from having a chatbot. That's a massive target market.

To access these channels, we can click on **Channels** in the Lex editor. We can start by selecting Facebook as the channel and then giving this channel a name and description. Next, we can select the alias that we want to deploy. Make sure that you've published your chatbot to an alias and then we can select one of them in the dropdown:

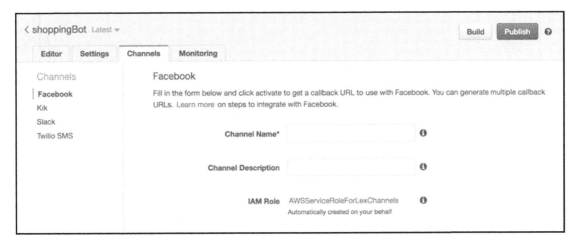

Channels in Lex console

The last thing we can do right now is choose a **Verify Token**. This is a string that we will use later to help connect Facebook to our Lex chatbot. This can be any string of letters and numbers you like.

The **Page Access Token** and **App Secret Key** are two values that we'll get once we've created a Facebook app, so we'll do this next.

# Creating and connecting a Facebook Messenger app

To integrate a chatbot into Facebook Messenger, we need to first create a Facebook app. To get started, go to `https://developers.facebook.com/` and click **Log In**. If this is your first Facebook app, then you'll need to link this developer account to your personal account. Once you've logged in, you can create your first app. Click **My Apps** and then select **Create New App**. This will open a popup where we can name the app.

This app name won't be displayed to users; it is only ever seen by Facebook page admins:

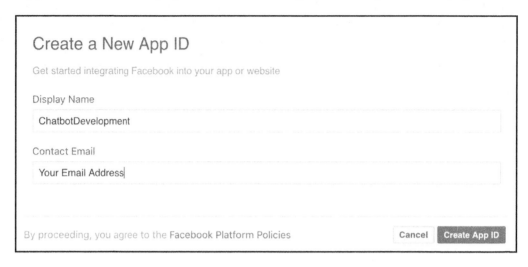

Creating your Facebook app

Facebook apps can be used to do a huge range of things, but we're wanting to build a Messenger chatbot, so we need to click **Set Up** under **Messenger**.

You should now be on a page titled **Messenger Platform,** and, on the left, you should see **Messenger** under **PRODUCTS**. The first thing we need to do is to create a token so that Lex can get access to this app. To generate the token, we can go to the **Token Generation** section and click the **Select a Page** dropdown:

Generating your page token

If you're not an admin on any Facebook pages, then you're going to have to create one. On Facebook itself, you can quickly and easily make a page for the fake shop or just a page for yourself as a developer.

When you select the page, a token will be generated. This can be copied and pasted into the **Page Access Token** field in our Lex channel configuration.

The last thing we need to get is the **App Secret** key, which we can find in our app page under **Settings** | **Basic**:

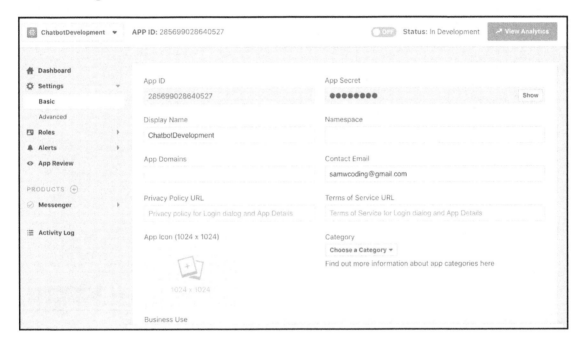

Getting app credentials

With all of the details of the channel now done, we can click **Activate,** and we'll be given a new **Callback URL**. Copy this URL and go back to our Facebook app screen. Go back to the Messenger config **Messenger** | **Settings** in the left-hand menu, and scroll down to **Webhooks**. Webhooks are how Facebook is going to send messages through to our Lex chatbot.

Click **Setup Webhooks** to open a popup where we can paste the URL we got from Lex as the **Callback URL** and then the **Verify Token** that we specified in the setup of the Lex channel. We also need to subscribe to **messages**, **messaging_postbacks**, and **messaging_optins**. These options are selecting which types of messages Facebook will send to Lex:

| New Page Subscription | | ✕ |
|---|---|---|
| **Callback URL** | | |
| Validation requests and Webhook notifications for this object will be sent to this URL. | | |
| **Verify Token** | | |
| Token that Facebook will echo back to you as part of callback URL verification. | | |
| **Subscription Fields** | | |
| ☐ messages | ☐ messaging_postbacks | ☐ messaging_optins |
| ☐ message_deliveries | ☐ message_reads | ☐ messaging_payments |
| ☐ messaging_pre_checkouts | ☐ messaging_checkout_updates | ☐ messaging_account_linking |
| ☐ messaging_referrals | ☐ message_echoes | ☐ messaging_game_plays |
| ☐ standby | ☐ messaging_handovers | ☐ messaging_policy_enforcement |
| Learn more | | |
| | Cancel | Verify and Save |

Facebook Webhook options

Clicking **Verify and Save** will send a request to Lex and will expect the correct verify token to be sent back. Normally, you would have to set up that endpoint, but Lex handles all of this.

The last Webhook setup that we need to do is to select the page we can subscribe to. In the **Webhooks** section, there's a **Select a Page** dropdown, which you need to set and then click **Subscribe**.

Now the chatbot should be on your page, but it'll only be accessible by yourself and other people who you've added to the app. Adding more people to test or work on the app can be done in the **Roles** menu on the left.

At this point, you can test out your chatbot by going to your Facebook page and sending it a message. Lex should receive the message and send the correct response as it did in the Lex console.

Before you can set your new app live, you need to ask Facebook to allow you to do page messaging. This is done by scrolling to the bottom of the **Messenger** settings page and adding **pages_messaging** to the submission. At this point, you will probably be asked to complete a few more things such as adding an app icon and setting a privacy policy URL and category:

## Current Submission

 **pages_messaging**

Complete the <u>details</u> for this item before submitting.

**Before you can submit for review, complete the following:**

- Complete each of the items above.
- Your app must have App Icon (1024 x 1024) set. Please visit Settings to add one.
- Your app must have Privacy Policy URL set. Please visit Settings to add one.
- Your app must have Category set. Please visit Settings to add one.
- Your app must have Business Use set. Please visit Settings to add one.

Submission requirements

Once you've completed these, you can submit your app for review. You'll be asked to provide example commands and their automated responses. Make sure that you've tested the commands before submitting as it can take up to a week to get an app verified, so getting it right the first time is key.

Facebook has recently updated its policies so that to activate your chatbot you need to have an approved Facebook business account. This involves registering your business details and providing a few pieces of evidence.

Once your app and the connected business account are verified, you get the joy of switching it from **OFF** to **ON** and allowing everyone to start messaging your chatbot.

# Slack

Slack is a messaging platform massively popular with software developers and tech companies, and it fully supports chatbots.

As we did with Facebook, we need to choose a **Channel Name** and **Alias,** and you can provide a **Channel Description** if you want to.

## Creating and connecting a Slack app

To start setting up our Slack app, we need to log in to the Slack API (`https://api.slack.com/`). Once we're logged in, we can create a new app:

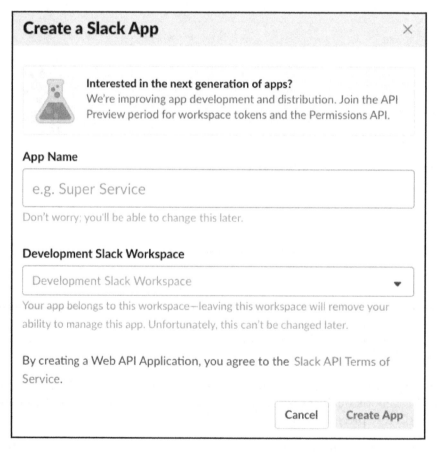

Create Slack app

Next, we can set up the features for the app, which for us is configuring the bots feature. We need to give our app a **Display name** and a **Default username**, and sett the **Always On** toggle to **On**. This means that the bot will always appear to be online.

With this set up, we can now go to **Basic Information** in the left-hand menu, where we can get the **Client ID**, **Client Secret**, and **Verification Token,** which we can paste into our Lex channel configuration.

When you **Activate** the Lex channel, you should get a **Postback URL** and **OAuth URL**. The **Postback URL** is the URL that listens for messages from Slack and the **OAuth URL** is used to authenticate your bot.

With the **OAuth URL**, we can go back to `api.Slack.com` and navigate into our app. From here, we can navigate to **OAuth & Permissions** in the left-hand menu and click **Add New Redirect URL**. We can now paste the **OAuth URL** that we got from Lex.

We also need to set the scope of permissions that this app will get. In the **Scopes** section, we can add permissions by selecting from the **Select Permission Scopes** dropdown. We need to add **Send messages as ... (chat:write:bot)** and **Access information about your workspace (team: read)** and then save the changes:

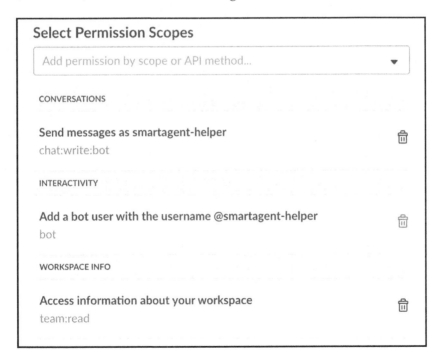

Slack permissions

The next step is to allow Lex to interact with our Slack app by clicking on **Interactive Components** in the left-hand menu and turning **Interactivity** on. We can then set the **Request URL** to the **Postback URL** that we got from a Lex activation.

The last step is to enable **Event Subscriptions,** which can be found in the menu on the left. Turn it **On,** and paste our **Postback URL** as the **Request URL,** and click **Add Workspace Event**. Scroll down until you see **message.im,** and add it, before saving changes.

To install our app onto your Slack channel, we need to go to **Manage Distribution** and click **Add to Slack**. You should be redirected to your Slack team, and you should see our chatbot in the **Direct Messages**. If you don't see it, you can search for it using the **+** icon.

You can now send messages to the chatbot through Slack and you should receive the same responses as we got when we tested in the Lex console.

# Twilio

**Twilio** is a platform that allows you to use SMS, calls, and video calls to interact with users. We're going to be using it to allow users to interact with our bot over SMS text messages.

As we did with the two previous integrations, we can give the channel a *name* and *choose an alias*. The **Account SID** and **Authentication Token** need to be got from Twilio, so that's what we'll do now.

## Creating and connecting Twilio

To get started, we need to go to www.twilio.com and sign up or log in. Once you've signed in, go to **Settings** in the left-hand menu and, under **API Credentials,** you will see **ACCOUNT SID** and **AUTH TOKEN**. These can be copied and pasted into the Lex channel setup, and then we can click **Activate**. Copy the **Endpoint URL** that is generated and go back to the Twilio console.

In the console, we need to go to **Programmable SMS** and we start by getting a number from which we can text:

Getting a number

We'll be given a random phone number, and we can either **Choose this Number** or **Search for a different number:**

Choosing a number

Now that we have a phone number to use, we can select **Messaging Services** from the menu on the left. We can then add a service for our Lex chatbot. This service will allow us to receive text messages and pass them through to our Lex chatbot before replying with the Lex response. Give the service a name and make sure to set the use case to **Chat Bot/Interactive 2-Way**:

Creating a new service

You should be sent to the **Numbers** sub-menu, where we can **Add an Existing Number** to this service. This selects the number that our chatbot will use. Select the number that we chose earlier and add this to the service.

With the number set on the service, we can go to **Configure** to add the Endpoint URL that we get from Lex. We want to be able to receive inbound messages, so click the **PROCESS INBOUND MESSAGES** tickbox and paste our URL in the **REQUEST URL** box. Save this service, and we have just one thing left to do to: get our SMS chatbot working:

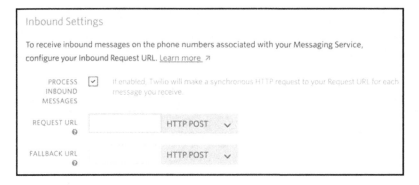

Inbound settings

The last thing we need to do is to allow our Twilio to send SMS messages to numbers in our region. Inside the **Messaging Services,** go to **Settings** and then **Geo Permissions**. This is a list of all of the country locations that are available; we need to activate our regions to allow us to test it.

Search for your country and activate it by ticking the checkbox. You can activate as many regions as you like.

You can now test out your chatbot by sending a text to the number you chose for this service:

Texting chatbot

If you want to get rid of the **Sent from your Twilio trial account** message, then you'll need to upgrade.

# HTTP endpoint

It's great that Lex makes it so easy to integrate our chatbot into Facebook, Slack, and Twilio, but we might also want to have our chatbot integrate into other services that don't have built-in integrations. For this, we can create an API endpoint for sending messages to our Lex chatbot.

With AWS, we are lucky that they let you create an API with Lambdas and API Gateway. This means that we don't need to run a server, which means less work for us.

# Creating the Lambda

We start by creating a new folder in our Lambdas repository called `lex-shopping-api` with an `index.js` file inside. In this file, we can start by exporting a handler that checks that the event was a `POST` request and calls `sendToLex` to generate a reply. This reply then gets passed to `done` which formats the data, so it can be returned to API Gateway:

```
exports.handler = async (event) => {
    if (event.httpMethod === "POST") {
        let reply = await sendToLex(event);
        return done(reply);
    }
};
```

We now need to create the `sendToLex` function. The first thing that this function needs to do is to map the event body into the format that Lex requires. We'll create this `mapMessageToLex` function later:

```
const sendToLex = async event => {
    console.log('event', event);
    let messageForLex = mapMessageToLex(JSON.parse(event.body));
}
```

This message now needs to be sent to Lex. Amazon has made this easy by creating the Lex runtime, which allows you to send messages to your Lex chatbots. To access the Lex runtime, we need to install the `aws-sdk` by running `npm init` and `npm install --save aws-sdk` inside our `lex-shopping-api` folder. We can then require it in and create a new instance of the Lex runtime class by adding this code at the top of our file:

```
const AWS = require('aws-sdk');
const lexruntime = new AWS.LexRuntime();
```

To post a message to Lex, we need to call `lexruntime.postText()`, passing in the `messageForLex` and a handler callback. We can wrap the whole thing in a `new Promise` to allow us to control the `async` flow better:

```
let lexPromise = new Promise((resolve, reject) => {
    lexruntime.postText(messageForLex, (err, data) => {
        if (err) {
            reject(err);
        } else {
            resolve(data);
        }
    })
});
```

We can now `await` the `lexPromise` using our error handler to get either the response or an error. If there is an error, then we can return that error, and if we get a response, we can set the `res` to be an object containing the message:

```
let [err, res] = await to(lexPromise);
if (err) {
    return { err }
}
console.log('lex response', res);
return { res: { message: res.message } }
```

These returned values will flow all the way back to populate the reply variable in our handler. This gets passed to `done`, so we now need to create that function. API Gateway expects to get a response in a specific format so this function is returning that format:

```
const done = ({ err, res }) => {
    console.log('res', res);
    console.log('error', err);
    return {
        statusCode: err ? '404' : '200',
        body: err ? JSON.stringify({ error: err }) : JSON.stringify(res),
        headers: {
            'Content-Type': 'application/json',
            'Access-Control-Allow-Methods': '*',
            'Access-Control-Allow-Origin': '*'
        },
    };
}
```

The last function that we need to create is `mapMessageToLex`. Lex runtime requires that it gets an object with `botAlias`, `botName`, `inputText`, `userId`, and `sessionAttributes` so we map the message into this format. If you want to create an API for a different bot, then all you need to do is to change the `botName` and `botAlias`:

```
const mapMessageToLex = message => {
    return {
        botAlias: 'prod',
        botName: 'shoppingBot',
        inputText: message.text,
        userId: message.sessionID,
        sessionAttributes: {}
    };
}
```

# Testing

To test that this Lambda works properly, we can run some tests on it. The only values that need to be passed into this Lambda are the `body` and `httpMethod`. Because the `body` is a string, we need to escape the quotation marks:

```
{
    "body": "{\"text\":\"I want to buy a shirt\", \"sessionID\":
\"abc123\"}",
    "httpMethod": "POST"
}
```

Running this test should result in this response, which is in the format that API Gateway expects:

```
{
    "statusCode": "200",
    "body": "{\"message\":\"What size of shirt are you looking for?\"}",
    "headers": {
        "Content-Type": "application/json",
        "Access-Control-Allow-Methods": "*",
        "Access-Control-Allow-Origin": "*"
    }
}
```

# Connecting API Gateway

API Gateway is a service that allows us to create URLs that can accept all of the normal API request methods. Start by going to the API Gateway service in AWS and clicking **Get Started**.

When creating our first API, we should select **New API** and then we can give this API a name and **Description**, and click **Create API**:

Create new API

In Amazon API Gateway, an API refers to a collection of resources and methods that can be invoked through HTTPS endpoints.

◉ **New API**    ○ **Clone from existing API**    ○ **Import from Swagger**    ○ **Example API**

Settings

Choose a friendly name and description for your API.

| | |
|---|---|
| **API name*** | LexbotAPI |
| **Description** | An API for accessing Lex |
| **Endpoint Type** | Regional    ↕ ❶ |

**\* Required**

[ Create API ]

New API

You should now be on the configuration page for your API, but there are currently no endpoints created. Click on the **Actions** dropdown and select **Create Resource**. Doing this allows you to have the APIs for all of your Lex chatbots on a similar URL:

Creating a resource

Name the resource `shopping-bot` and click **Create Resource**:

## New Child Resource

Use this page to create a new child resource for your resource. ⦿

| | |
|---|---|
| **Configure as** ⧉proxy resource | ☐ ❶ |
| **Resource Name*** | shopping-bot |
| **Resource Path*** | / shopping-bot |

You can add path parameters using brackets. For example, the resource path **{username}** represents a path parameter called 'username'. Configuring /{proxy+} as a proxy resource catches all requests to its sub-resources. For example, it works for a GET request to /foo. To handle requests to /, add a new ANY method on the / resource.

| | |
|---|---|
| **Enable API Gateway CORS** | ☐ ❶ |

**\* Required**    Cancel    **Create Resource**

New resource

Now that we have a resource created, we can attach a method to it. In our Lambda, we check that the `httpMethod` is `POST` so we need to create a `POST` method. Click on our `shopping-bot` resource and click **Actions | Create Method**:

New method

This will open the method setup window, and there are a lot of ways to configure your method, but we're going to call our API Lambda. Make sure the integration type is **Lambda Function** and that **Use Lambda Proxy integration** is ticked. This makes sure that all of the request data is proxied through to the Lambda.

The next thing in the method setup is to select our `lex-shopping-api` as the Lambda function and to **Save** the method:

Method setup

Finally, we need to add **cross-origin resource sharing (CORS)** to our API. This allows us to access our API from different internet browsers. This will be important when we build a frontend for this API in the next section. Select our **shopping-bot** resource, and then we can click **Actions | Enable CORS**. We can leave all of the settings as default and click **Enable CORS and replace existing CORS headers**, confirming that we want to replace existing values:

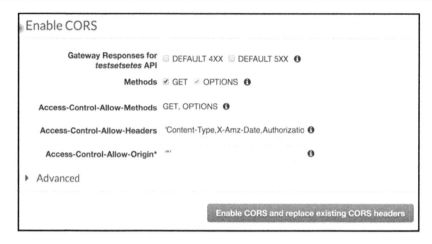

Adding CORS

# Testing

We can now test that our Lambda is being called properly by selecting the **POST** method and clicking on **TEST**:

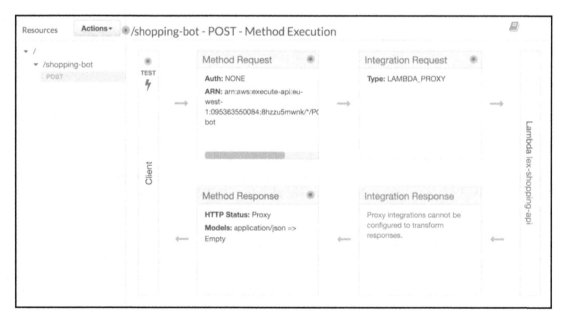

Method TEST

In this screen, we can set query strings, headers, and the request body. We don't need to send any query strings or headers, so we can scroll straight down to the request body section. As we should remember from the testing of the Lambda, all we need to pass through in the body is the `text` and a `sessionID`, so this is what we can put as the request body:

```
{
    "text":"I want to buy a shirt",
    "sessionID": "abc123"
}
```

When we hit **Test**, API Gateway will send our request through to our Lambda. Our Lambda will send it to our Lex chatbot and will send back the response. Our response body should come back like this:

```
{
    "message": "What size of shirt are you looking for?"
}
```

# Building the API

The last thing to do is to build our API. While on our API, we can select **Actions | Deploy API**. As this is the first time we are deploying this API, we need to create a new stage. Give your stage a name and description, and you can also add a deployment description before clicking **Deploy**:

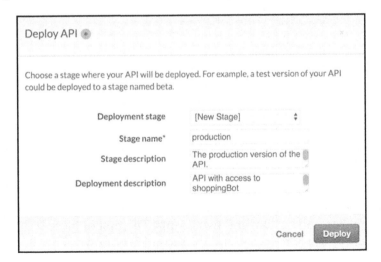

Creating a stage

When your API deploys, you'll be given a URL for it, which will be `https://{unique-code}.execute-api.eu-west-1.amazonaws.com/{stage-name}`. To access the endpoint that we made, we need to add `/shopping-bot` to the end. For example, `https://acffds-4fnf8x-se54fws-s34d.execute-api.eu-west-1.amazonaws.com/production/shopping-bot`. This now means you can use this API to integrate Lex into a wider range of systems.

# Web user interface

Having our own chatbot interface allows users to access it by going to a web page, but we can also integrate that into other websites, or even create mobile apps for our chatbot. We can use the API that we created to easily access the chatbot without making our AWS credentials public.

# HTML

To start, we need an HTML page to build upon. The three components that we need to start are a message area, a typing input box, and a send button. Create a folder with an `index.html` file inside and we can add this code to that file:

```
<!DOCTYPE html>
<html lang="en">
<head>
    <link rel="stylesheet" href="./style.css">
</head>
<body>
    <div id="messageArea"></div>
    <div id="inputDivs">
        <input type="text" id="textInput">
        <button id="sendButton">Send</button>
    </div>
</body>
<script src="https://unpkg.com/axios/dist/axios.min.js"></script>
<script src="./script.js"></script>
</html>
```

This is a simple HTML file that has a CSS link in the header so we can style our page, the message area, input box and button, and two scripts. The first of these scripts imports `axios` so we can easily make requests, and the second is our own script.

As we've included the `style.css` and `script.js` files, we should create these files in our folder.

# Creating our script

All of the functionality of this UI needs to be handled in this script file. When all of the HTML has loaded, we need to listen for the user clicking the **Send** button. When that happens, we need to get the text from the input box and write it as a sent message before sending it to our API. When our API replies, we can add the response as a received message.

To start, we need to make sure that the document has fully loaded. We can check if the document is ready, and if not, then we wait for the DOMContentLoaded event:

```
if (document.readyState === 'complete') {
    start();
} else {
    document.addEventListener("DOMContentLoaded", start())
}
```

We can now create the start function and set the API URL and session ID. We can use the Math.random() technique to make a random 16-digit number for the sessionID:

```
function start() {
    const URL = 'YOUR-API-URL/production/shopping-bot';
    // create unique code for this session
    const sessionID = Math.random().toString().slice(-16);
}
```

At the start() function, we also need to access the message area, text input box, and send button, using document.querySelector:

```
let messageArea = document.querySelector('#messageArea');
let textArea = document.querySelector('#textInput');
let sendButton = document.querySelector('#sendButton');
```

On to the sendButton, we can attach a listener for when the user clicks send. This will start by getting the value of the text input box. If there isn't any text then we can return nothing from the function:

```
sendButton.addEventListener('click', async e => {
    let text = textArea.value;
    console.log(text);
    if (!text) return;
}
```

If there is any text, then we can carry on to create a `sendElement` and add it to the message area. We need to make sure to add the classes of `sendMessage` and `message` to the element so we can style them later:

```
// Add to sent messages
let sendElement = document.createElement('div');
sendElement.classList.add('sendMessage');
sendElement.classList.add('message');
sendElement.appendChild(document.createTextNode(text));
messageArea.appendChild(sendElement);
```

Next, we have to send the message to our API. We can use `axios` as we imported it in the HTML file, passing through `text` and `sessionID` as the body. We need to make sure to copy the function from our Lambdas for error-handling here:

```
// send to the API
let [err, response] = await to(axios.post(URL, { text, sessionID }));
```

If there is an error in the response, then we can set the message to an apology; otherwise, it will be the `response.data.message`:

```
let responseMessage;
if (err) {
    responseMessage = 'Sorry I appear to have had an error';
} else {
    responseMessage = response.data.message;
}
```

The last thing to do is to add the received message to the message area so the user can see it. Don't forget to add the `receivedMessage` and `message` classes for styling later:

```
// adding the response to received messages
let receiveElement = document.createElement('div');
receiveElement.classList.add('receivedMessage');
receiveElement.classList.add('message');
receiveElement.appendChild(document.createTextNode(responseMessage));
messageArea.appendChild(receiveElement);
```

If we open the HTML document in a browser, now we should be able to type and send messages to our Lex chatbot:

i want to buy a shirt
What size of shirt are you looking for?
large
What colour would you like?
red
There are 4 red shirt in stock. Would you like to add one to your basket?
Send

Basic messaging

# Styling the frontend

We've created an awesome web page that allows users to talk to a chatbot, but, currently, it looks awful. We can fix this by using our CSS file. While building the chat, we've been adding classes and IDs to the elements. This means we can set styles on those classes and ids to style our whole chat window. The first thing to do is to set the size of the message area. We can also add a light background and set the overflow to scroll:

```
#messageArea {
    height: 93vh;
    max-width: 450px;
    background: #eee;
    overflow-y: scroll;
}
```

Next, we can style the messages. We add common styling to the message class such as the padding, margin, and max-width, while the alignment, background, and border-radius are defined on each type of message:

```
.message {
    padding: 3%;
    margin: 2%;
    position: relative;
    max-width: 70%;
}
.sendMessage {
    right: -20%;
    background: blue;
```

```
        color: white;
        border-radius: 16px 16px 8px 16px
    }
    .receivedMessage {
        background: #bbb;
        left: 0;
        border-radius: 16px 16px 16px 8px;
    }
```

The last bit to style is the input textbox and send button. We can use display: flex on the container div and flex-grow: 2 on the text input so that it stretches to fill the width left by the button. We can style the button up a bit with a different border and background:

```
    #inputDivs {
        width: 450px;
        display: flex;
    }
    #textInput {
        font-size: 15px;
        flex-grow: 2;
    }
    #sendButton {
        font-size: 15px;
        border: 0px solid lightskyblue;
        background: lightskyblue;
        border-radius: 8px;
        padding: 8px;
        margin-left: 8px;
    }
```

This results in a much nicer user experience than the plain text we had before. This is where you can spend some time customizing the look of your interface to be exactly how you want it to be.

You can even style this to match the brand colors of a company:

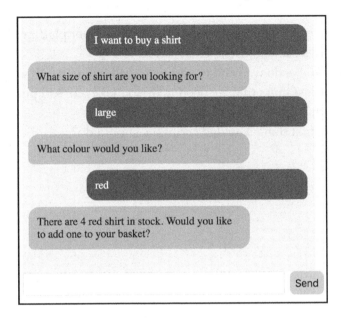

Styled chat

# Summary

In this chapter, we've learned how to create integrations that allow users to access our chatbots from Facebook Messenger, Slack, and Twilio.

We've also learned how to create an API to give us the ability to integrate our chatbots into other services that Amazon doesn't currently support. This API used a Lambda function to handle the requests sent through API Gateway.

We then used this API to create a frontend web page for our chatbot. We wrote a simple HTML document and then used a script to communicate with the API and add the messages to the page. The last thing we did was add styling to the page so that it looked like a real messaging platform.

# Questions

1. Why do we want to integrate our chatbots into other platforms and services?
2. What services can you use to create an API?
3. What two things do we need to add to an API before it will work?
4. What is the last thing that we need to do to make our API public?
5. Name the three parts of our chatbot web page.
6. What is the first thing a loaded script file should do?

# Improving the User Experience for Your Bots

# 8

After having learned how to create Alexa Skills and Lex chatbots, we will now learn how we can improve the user experience. This is important, as adding images to your Lex chatbot or having a better voice model for Alexa can make a huge difference to whether the user enjoys interacting with your chatbot. Adding these features will also make your chatbots stand out from the basic, text-only chatbots.

The following topics will be covered in this chapter:

- Adding response cards to Lex chatbots
- Using phrase slots to create a more refined voice model for Alexa Skills
- Using utterance monitoring with Amazon Lex to refine interaction models

# Technical requirements

In this chapter, we will be modifying our existing Lambda functions, so we'll be deploying them using the local development setup that we created `Chapter 2`, *Getting Started with AWS and Amazon CLI.*

All of the code and data required for this chapter can be found at `http://bit.ly/chatbot-ch8`.

# Response cards in Amazon Lex

Cards give you a way to offer a richer in-conversation experience than just text messages by integrating buttons, images, and more. Cards can be used for many purposes, such as displaying product information, asking the message recipient to choose from a predetermined set of options, and showing search results. If you are integrating your cards into Slack or Facebook, then they will be shown on those platforms:

Example cards in Facebook

# Creating a card

To create a card, we need to change the format of the response that we are sending back to Lex. This means we need to change the functions in LexResponses by passing in a responseCard attribute. We can then add this responseCard to the dialogAction object. If we don't pass in a response card parameter, we still want the function to work so we default it to null:

```
elicitIntent({ message, sessionAttributes = {}, responseCard = null }) {
  return {
    sessionAttributes,
    dialogAction: {
      type: 'ElicitIntent',
      message: { contentType: 'PlainText', content: message },
      responseCard
    },
  };
}
```

This needs to be done for elicitSlot, close, elicitIntent, and confirmIntent, but not for delegate as that function doesn't send messages.

To add a response card, we need to make sure that the response is also in the correct format. To make this easier for ourselves, we can make a new function inside LexResponses called createCardFormat. This will take a single attribute of cards, which is an array of objects containing a title, subtitle, imageUrl, linkUrl, and buttons:

```
createCardFormat(cards) {
  return {
    version: 1,
    contentType: "application/vnd.amazonaws.card.generic",
    genericAttachments: cards.map(({ title, subtitle, imageUrl, linkUrl,
buttons }) => {
      return {
        title,
        subtitle,
        imageUrl,
        attachmentLinkUrl: linkUrl,
        buttons: buttons.map(({ text, value }) => {
          return { text, value };
        })
      };
    })
  }
}
```

# Using cards in chats

With our modified `LexResponses` class, we can now start adding cards to our existing Lex Lambdas. One obvious place to use cards is in the shopping app to display the items we found based on the user's search. This means we are going to alter our `productFind` Lambda.

After we create the message telling the user how many of the items we have in stock (line 77 of `productFind/index.js`), we can create our first card.

This is going to be a single card with a title of the item, a subtitle of the stock, an image, and `Add to Cart` and `Not Now` buttons:

```
let responseCard = Lex.createCardFormat([{
    title: `${size}, ${colour}${type === 'trousers' ? ', ' + length :
''}${type}`,
    subTitle: `${item.stock} in stock`,
    imageUrl: item.imageUrl,
    buttons: [
        { text: 'Add to Cart', value: 'Yes' },
        { text: 'Not Now', value: 'No' }]
    }
]);
```

As you can see, we are giving the buttons a different value to their text. This allows the response we receive to be different from the button that the user clicks.

You may have noticed that we have also added an image using `item.imageURL` but this never existed in our original data. We need to go through and add this to each of the items in the stock data. Luckily, we can use the same image for the different sizes of clothes. The stock data with images is available to download at `bit.ly/chatbot-ch8`.

When we deploy these changes, we can test it out in the Lex chat window. We can go through the normal `productFind` flow up to the point where we are shown the product selected. When we are told how many are in stock, we are also shown a card displaying the information:

Chat card

If we have the Facebook or Slack integrations hooked up from the previous chapters, then our new cards should work on there too. Lex does a lot of clever logic to translate the card into the correct format needed for each platform and then uses them in the replies. It should be noted that Facebook crops the images to a 1:1.9 ratio, so selecting your images with that in mind is a good idea:

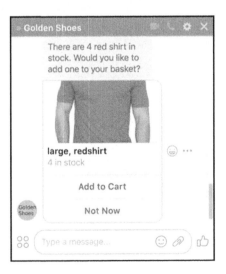

Facebook card

# Alexa search queries

Alexa is great when you know the sort of responses that your users are going to be saying, but what if they ask for something you aren't expecting? Even using custom slot types can be limiting, which could result in a user's request being incorrectly handled. Luckily, Amazon has introduced the **Search Query** slot type.

This slot type for Alexa is designed to be able to take a much wider range of values so that you can handle more requests.

We're going to add a new intent onto our existing Weather Gods skill that uses a **Search Query** slot type to allow users to search for places in a city. We'll be using Google Maps API to power the backend.

Go to your Alexa developer's console and open the `WeatherGods` skill. Add a new intent called `searchIntent` and we can start by creating the different slots that we'll be using. Create two slots, one called `query` and the other called `city`. Our query slot can be given a slot type of **AMAZON.SearchQuery** and our city slot will be **AMAZON.US_CITY**:

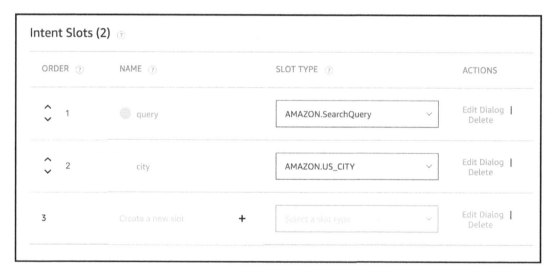

Search slots

With the slots completed, we can start populating the utterances. Unfortunately, we can't have a search query slot in an utterance with another slot so we'll have to fill one slot at a time. We should allow a user to ask about a city or ask a query to start the intent:

## Sample Utterances (6) ⑦

What might a user say to invoke this intent?

What is there to see in  {city}

search for a  {query}

What is in  {city}

does  {query}

is there a  {query}

Utterances for search query

Now that we have our slots and utterances completed, we can modify our existing `weatherGods` Lambda to handle the new intent. Find the Lambda in your editor, open the `index.js` file, and go into the `handlers` object.

Inside the `handlers` object, we need to add a new handler called `searchIntent`. This handler will start by getting the city and query slot values and checking whether they exist. If they don't, we'll ask the user to tell us the missing information. We check `cityValue` first, so we can specify the city when we ask for the query:

```
const SearchHandler = {
    canHandle(handlerInput) {
        return handlerInput.requestEnvelope.request.type ===
'IntentRequest' &&
            handlerInput.requestEnvelope.request.intent.name ===
'searchIntent';
    },
    async handle(handlerInput) {
        const { slots } = handlerInput.requestEnvelope.request.intent;
```

```
let { city, query } = slots;
let cityValue = city.value;
let queryValue = query.value;
if (!cityValue) {
    let slotToElicit = 'city';
    let speechOutput = `What city are you looking in?`;
    return handlerInput.responseBuilder
        .speak(speechOutput)
        .addElicitSlotDirective(slotToElicit)
        .getResponse();
}
if (!queryValue) {
    let slotToElicit = 'query';
    let speechOutput = `What are you looking for in ${cityValue}`;
    return handlerInput.responseBuilder
        .speak(speechOutput)
        .addElicitSlotDirective(slotToElicit)
        .getResponse();
}
    }
  }
}
```

If we have both the city and query values, then we can use these to make a request to Google's Maps API.

# Google Cloud Platform

To use Google Maps API, we need to set up a Google Cloud Platform developers account. We can get one by going to cloud.google.com/ and clicking **Try free**. You need to sign in to a Google account, confirm terms and conditions, and then enter payment information. Don't worry; you get $300 of free credit when you start, so you shouldn't get billed any time soon.

To start, we need to create a project by clicking **Select a project** in the upper-left corner and then choosing **NEW PROJECT**. Now we can name our new project WeatherGodsAPI and click **CREATE**.

With our project created, we need to check that it is selected in the upper-left corner of the page and then we can start to set up this project. In the search box, we can search for `Places API` and enable it for this project:

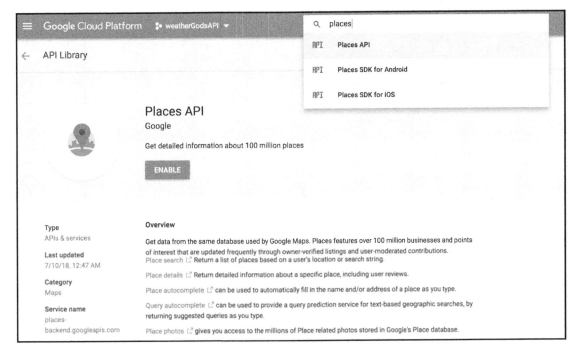

Places API

Once the **Places API** has been enabled on this project, we need to generate an API key so we can access it from our Lambda. Click on **Credentials** and, from the **Create Credentials** drop-down menu, select **API Key**:

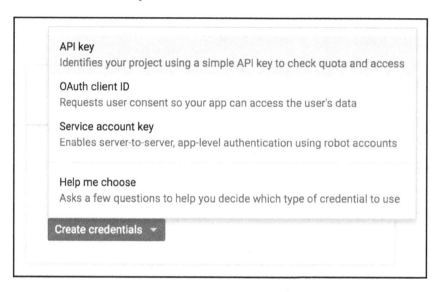

API key
Identifies your project using a simple API key to check quota and access

OAuth client ID
Requests user consent so your app can access the user's data

Service account key
Enables server-to-server, app-level authentication using robot accounts

Help me choose
Asks a few questions to help you decide which type of credential to use

**Create credentials** ▼

Creating an API key

You need to copy this API key, as we'll be using it in our Lambda.

# Continuing Lambda building

We now have an API key that we can use to hit the Google Places API. Copy it and open your Lambda in the Lambda console. Scroll down to **Environment variables,** and create a new variable with a key of **GOOGLE_API_KEY,** and paste the API key as the value. Make sure not to remove the other API key, which is for `openWeatherMaps`:

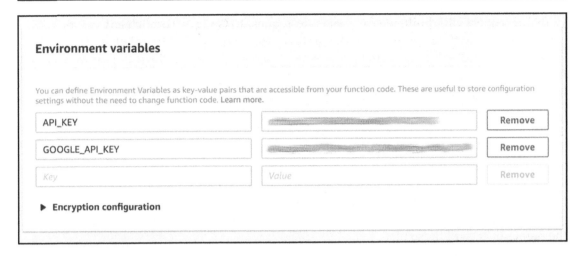

Storing environment variables

With our Google API key stored as an environment variable, we can create our request that we'll be sending to Google. The format of the API request URL is this:

```
https://maps.googleapis.com/maps/api/place/findplacefromtext/json?input={YO
UR SEARCH}&inputtype=textquery&fields=formatted_address,name&key={YOUR API
KEY}
```

To make it easier for ourselves, we can store most sections of this as constants, even the Google API key. In our index.js file, we can add these constants to the top of the file:

```
const GOOGLE_API_KEY = process.env.GOOGLE_API_KEY;
const googleURL =
'https://maps.googleapis.com/maps/api/place/findplacefromtext/json?input=';
const queryString =
'&inputtype=textquery&fields=formatted_address,name&key=';
```

With these constants accessible, the only part that we need to generate is our search. To do this, we can take our queryValue and our cityValue and turn it into a search phrase. This can be done by joining {queryValue} and {cityValue} into a basic sentence. Because we are inserting this into a URL, we need to use %20 instead of spaces and then we can build our request:

```
let completeURL = googleURL + [queryValue, 'in', cityValue].join('%20') +
queryString + GOOGLE_API_KEY;
```

With our request URL built, we can make our request to Google. To catch any errors, we can use our `to` method and then check that there are no errors and that there is a `response.data` field. If we didn't get what we expect, we can tell the user that we couldn't find that information:

```
if (err || !res || !res.data) {
    let apology = `unfortunately I couldn't find that for you`;
    return handlerInput.responseBuilder
        .speak(apology)
        .getResponse();
}
```

If our request did successfully return some data, then we can build a response for the user. First, we can tell them how many of their query there are in that city, and then we can list the names of each of those places:

```
let data = res.data;
let info = `There's ${data.candidates.length}
${query.value}${data.candidates.length === 1 ? "" : 's'} in ${city.value}.
${data.candidates.map(candidate => `the ${candidate.name}`)}`;
return handlerInput.responseBuilder
    .speak(info)
    .withShouldEndSession(false)
    .getResponse();
```

We've now completed our updated Lambda and can deploy it to AWS using our build script from Chapter 2, *Getting Started with AWS and Amazon CLI*.

# Rebuilding the skill and testing

Back in our skill in the Alexa Console, we can check our modified skill and make sure to save it and rebuild it. When it has finished building, we can click **Test** to try it out. You can test the old intents that we built in Chapter 4, *Connecting your Alexa Skill to External APIs*, and they should all work as before, but we really want to test our new intent.

You can now ask the weather gods what there is in Manchester and say that you're looking for a Catholic cathedral, and your skill will ask Google for Catholic cathedral in Manchester. It should tell you there is one called Salford Cathedral.

While this is good, we could have used a custom slot type and listed lots of things that a user might ask for. This is where search queries are really useful: they can handle far less common requests. We can ask for Saint Paul's primary school in Manchester, and we'll get a result. There is no way we could have created a custom slot that would be large enough to include every school name:

Testing search query

# Lex utterance monitoring

When you create your intents and generate the list of utterances, you try your best to cover everything that a user might say. Unfortunately, people often come up with unique ways of saying something that you've not thought of. In this case, the user will get an "*I don't understand*" message from Lex. This obviously isn't great for providing a good user experience.

Luckily, Lex has built-in monitoring to allow you to see the utterances that the users have been saying. To get to these, we need to click on the Monitoring tab in Lex. Lex utterances are stored for a specific chatbot version, so we need to select a value from the dropdown next to our chatbot name.

You should now have a screen of graphs showing the Lex usage. This can be useful, but we're looking for the tables of utterances, found in the menu on the left:

Utterance monitoring

You should now see a table with a toggle in the center for **Detected/Missed**. The **Detected** utterances can be useful for seeing how most of your users are interacting with the chatbot. This can help you work out which areas you can develop to improve your chatbot for the largest portion of your audience.

If you don't see any utterances, then there are a few things to check. You need to make sure that in the general settings of the chatbot, **COPPA** is set to **No**. Next, you should try changing the version of the chatbot (next to the chatbot name) as utterances are saved to a specific version. Utterances show up in these tables if they are between 24 hours and 15 days old. If you still don't see any utterances, then you may just need to wait until you have utterances within this range.

Utterance monitoring is very useful when users have said something that Lex couldn't match to one of your example utterances. The **Missed** utterances give you a list of all of the utterances where this has happened. Although some of them will be gibberish or typos, some of them will be valid utterances that you might not have thought about:

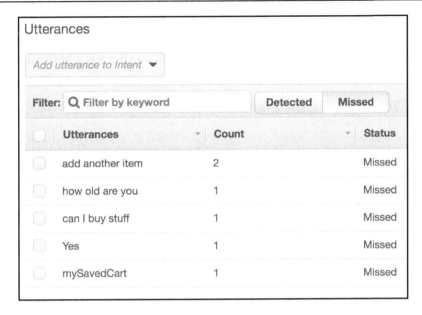

Missed utterances

Looking through the missed intents, you may realize that the user has typed an utterance that you hadn't thought of. You can easily add this to your intent by selecting the missed utterance and then selecting the intent from the dropdown that is just above the table. This saves manually copying and pasting the utterances into the intents.

Once you've moved all of the valid missed utterances into the correct intents, you need to make sure you build and deploy your updated chatbot.

# Summary

In this chapter, we've looked into three ways to improve the user experience of both Alexa Skills and Lex chatbots.

We started by creating cards in Lex chats to increase the visual information provided to a user. These cards are a great way to make your Lex chatbots stand out from just text-based chatbots.

We then moved over to Alexa, where we learned about **Search Query** slots. This slot type allows users to enter a wider range of values to fill a slot than we could allow using custom slot types.

The final tool we learned to use to improve the user experience was *utterance monitoring*. Seeing what your users are really saying to your chatbot helps you increase the example utterances for each intent. This results in a chatbot that can successfully handle a wider range of user utterances.

All of these things will provide more information or reduce the chance that the chatbots can't handle a user's requests.

In the final chapter we'll discuss a few of the best ways to continue your learning. We'll also talk about the future of chatbots and how they will become part of our everyday lives.

# Questions

1. What are the benefits of using cards in Lex conversations?
2. Do you need to use an image in a Lex card?
3. Why would you choose to use search query slot type over a default or custom slot type?
4. Can you populate a search query slot from the user utterance?
5. How can you find out which Lex utterances weren't matched to an intent?

# 9
# Review and Continued Development

Throughout this book, we've covered a wide range of topics and learned skills in lots of different areas. We've combined these skills to design and create complex chatbots on both the Alexa and Lex platforms.

This chapter will cover the following:

- Recap the skills that we've learned throughout this book
- Discuss how to continue your chatbot development exploration
- Discuss the future of chatbots

## What we've learned

There have been a lot of skills that have been covered in this book, both technical and non-technical.

## Conversation design

The first topic that was covered was conversation design. This is one of the most important sections of this book, as every good chatbot will need to go through this design stage. It doesn't matter whether it's going to be an Alexa Skill, Lex chatbot, or even a chatbot built using different technology.

When designing a chatbot, we always try to start with a perfect user conversation. Starting with a perfect conversation means that the users are likely to have the best possible experience with our chatbots.

Using the perfect conversation, we can start to build our flow diagrams. These provide more technical structure to the design, allowing us to specify what data we're saving, which APIs we're hitting, and triggering one flow from another. Creating a set of shorter flow diagrams that link together is incredibly powerful, as it provides flexibility to connect new entry points and features as the chatbot matures.

# Amazon Web Services

Next, we were introduced to **Amazon Web Services (AWS)** and the tools that we have access to. We started by creating an AWS Lambda using the Lambda console and then checked it using the built-in testing features.

Although creating Lambdas in the console is great for simple functions, we often need more functionality and a more reliable experience. We discussed the two other options—**Cloud9** and **local editing**—and we mentioned their advantages and their limitations.

Local editing had some great advantages but lacked the ability to easily create and update Lambdas. To fix this, we learned about the `aws-cli` and how we can use it to control our AWS products. Using the `aws-cli`, we created a build script that could take our local files, bundle them together, and deploy them to AWS. With this script, we now had a powerful development environment with easy deployment.

# Amazon Alexa

Then it was time to start building some chatbots. We started with Alexa and learned about the components that make up a chatbot. We learned to use intents, utterances, and slots to allow our users to interact with our chatbots.

To power this skill, we needed to create a Lambda to handle the requests. We used `alexa-sdk` to make it much easier to create the responses that we would be sending back to the user.

With a working Alexa Skill, we learned how to test it using the built-in testing tools. This way, we can test it as if we were a user, but with the ability to see how our skill is acting in the background.

Once we had tested the chatbot, we were ready to publish it. Alexa Skills need to be published to the Alexa Skill Store, and we learned how to follow this process to make our skills available to the public.

# Amazon S3

To increase the usefulness of all of our chatbots, we needed to be able to access large amounts of stored data. To do this, we learned how to create an S3 bucket, store data in it, and then access this data from our Lambdas. With this data access, we could provide users with a much larger amount of information on the topic that they requested.

# Using APIs

We then learned how to access third-party APIs to further improve the usefulness of our chatbots. We used the `openWeatherMaps` API as an example and this allowed us to access live information that we would never have been able to generate ourselves.

To do this, we also learned about `axios` and making API requests. With these skills, you'll be able to make requests to an API to add new features to your chatbots. We also looked at the two best ways to handle errors—using `try/catch` and the `to()` method. We discussed the reasons that you might want to use one or the other and why error handling is important.

# Amazon Lex

Building text-based chatbots came next as we learned about Amazon Lex. We saw the similarities and differences between Lex and Alexa, and we built on our existing knowledge to create our first Lex chatbots.

We learned that each intent can return a hardcoded response or trigger a Lambda. Being able to trigger a different Lambda from each intent allowed us to create lots of very customized Lambdas to do exactly what we wanted.

When we triggered a Lambda from Lex, it expected a very defined response format. Unfortunately, there isn't a `lex-sdk` yet, so we built our own. We saw five different response types and created methods for each of them. This allowed us to create the required responses much more easily.

# Dynamo DB

While S3 is great for storing large amounts of data that probably won't change very much, it isn't great for storing data that is regularly changing. To store this type of data, we learned about DynamoDB. This is Amazon's non-relational database, and it gives us the ability to easily store, access, and update information. We used this to store the shopping cart used for an online store.

We created a `Dynamo` class that had methods for getting, writing, updating, and deleting these Dynamo tables so that we didn't have to write the long and complex code needed every time.

# Publishing Lex chatbots

There's no point being able to build an amazing chatbot if your users can't access it. We learned to leverage the massive existing user bases of Facebook, Slack, and Twilio by integrating our chatbot into those platforms.

We also built an API service that allowed us to integrate our chatbot into a much wider range of applications. Building on this API, we created our own frontend interface for our chatbot. This was great, as it gave us the ability to make it look and work exactly how we wanted it to.

# Advanced features

The first seven chapters of this book taught us how to create powerful Alexa Skills and Lex chatbots by using other services such as S3, DynamoDB, and external APIs. In `Chapter 8`, *Improving User Experience for Your Bots*, we looked at some of the advanced features that are built into Lex and Alexa.

We first learned how to create information cards for Lex. This allowed us to send the user more visual information than the basic messages we were sending before. Adding these cards provided a huge boost to the user experience.

Then we learned about phrase slots in Alexa and how they can be used to capture information where the options that could be entered are too large to create a custom slot type. Being able to capture such a wide range of inputs into a slot makes our skills more reliable and robust.

The last thing that we learned about was utterance monitoring in Lex. This is where we can look at the utterances that Lex has detected and those that it has missed, which gives us an insight into the way that users are interacting with our chatbots. This also provides a mechanism to easily add utterances that we've missed to our existing intents.

# Continuing your learning

Now that you've completed this book, you have a great understanding of voice, and text-based chatbots. You're able to build complex, multi-flow chatbots that integrate other services such as S3, DynamoDB, and external APIs. If you've enjoyed learning how to build these systems, then you're in a great position to continue your journey.

There are a lot of different directions you can go with your learning, and I'll outline some possibilities for you—a few specific to Alexa or Lex, and then a few that would be great to learn for both Alexa and Lex.

# Alexa

If you really enjoyed building skills for Alexa, then there are two directions that I would go in with my learning.

## Amazon Echo Spot and Amazon Echo Show

The **Amazon Echo Spot** and **Amazon Echo Show** are Amazon's Alexa devices that also have screens. This means that you can provide users with visual information as well as voice responses. As with the cards on Lex, having that extra visual information can make the user experience much richer.

One big advantage of Echo devices with screens is that you can provide images to the user. Trying to tell a user about a product just using voice can be very hard but, with an image, the user experience is much smoother. You can also play videos, have a slideshow, or create custom displays with lots of varying information.

# Building a library of functions

If you enjoy building Alexa Skills and want to start building more of them, then there are going to be times when you want to use the same methods across multiple skills. There are two options—just copy the code every time, or create a library of method Lambdas. The first one is good for a small number of skills but will become annoying as you build more skills.

The second option will take longer to set up but will make building future skills much easier. The design for this setup is similar to the way that Lex works, where each intent triggers a single Lambda. Unfortunately, this isn't supported already, but we can create the same effect using the Lambda Invoke functions. This lets us trigger a Lambda from our `handlers` object.

The advantage of this method is that the common intents can trigger the same Lambda, reducing repeated code, whilst unique intents can still be built in the main handler Lambda.

# Lex

If you want to learn more skills specific to Lex, then the best direction would be learning to integrate it into more services.

There are hundreds of messaging services that Lex doesn't natively support, and being able to integrate your chatbot into these services would be a great skill to have. You could try integrating you chatbot into Telegram, Twitter, WeChat, or any other messaging services. To do this, you'll probably have to map the message into the correct format for that specific service. The mapping between formats can be quite tricky but is a great skill to learn.

Once you've built a mechanism to integrate Lex into these messaging platforms, you can advertise your integration or the fact that you can build a mechanism to integrate into the company's own messaging platform. Lots of companies want to be able to add chatbots to their existing messaging platform.

# Alexa and Lex

Continuing your learning with skills that can be used with both Alexa and Lex is probably the best use of your time, and there are many different directions to go in.

# Improving the build process

As you build more Alexa Skills and Lex chatbots, you will become frustrated with having to open the Alexa Skills Kit or the Lex console to add a new utterance or change an intent. Luckily, there is the `aws-cli` and `ask-cli` that we can use to build and update our skills and chatbots without having to go online.

You may remember the `aws-cli` from Chapter 2, *Getting Started with AWS and Amazon CLI*, where we used it to allow us to build Lambdas from our local machines. You can also use `aws-cli` to do something similar for Lex chatbots, whilst `ask-cli` has similar functionality for Alexa Skills. For both of these systems, there is quite a steep learning curve and you'll end up reading a lot of documentation, but being able to build a new chatbot or skill without ever using a browser is really useful.

You can either have the full structure of the chatbot or skill saved as a file on your computer, or you can create a system to generate these files based on a more simple config file. The advantage of the latter method is that the config files should be a lot easier to read and understand, making it a lot easier to figure out what needs to change for your update.

Once you've got this system in place, you should be able to create a new config file for a new bot within minutes. If you use this system, there is nothing stopping you from still using the online Alexa Skills Kit or Lex console to check, edit, and update your skills and chatbots.

If you are considering building chatbots or Alexa Skills as a job, then this tool will prove invaluable.

# Integrating more AWS services

In this book, we have learned how to use S3 and DynamoDB to improve the functionality of our skills and chatbots. There are currently over 100 AWS services, and some of them could be used to add even more functionality to your chatbots.

Here are a few ideas for service integrations:

- Amazon Redshift or Amazon ElastiCache, for a different method for database storage
- Amazon Cognito, for allowing users to sign in to access existing orders and chats or to provide results that are adjusted to match their user information
- Amazon Transcribe and Amazon Simple Email Service, to send the user an email with everything they said whilst chatting to Alexa

With the number of services available, what you can build and do with Alexa and Lex is limited only by your imagination.

## Integrating other APIs

The number of APIs available online is incredible! Just looking through one list of top APIs can give you some incredible ideas. What about a chatbot that you can ask about a certain product and it searches eBay for those products, allowing you to bid on it without leaving the chat! There's a census API that could be used to build an Alexa Skill where you can find out about the population, employment stats, economics, number of new houses, and much more about any area in the United States.

If you're looking to come up with some ideas for your own chatbots, then I highly recommend looking at APIs that are available and what you can do with them. You might find a function on one API that combines with a function on another API to create an immensely powerful chatbot.

# The future of chatbots

Chatbots have come a long way over the last decade and are now often found in households through Amazon Echo and Google Home. Technologically, they have improved in leaps and bounds, with improvements in AI and machine learning resulting in better language understanding as well as voice-to-text that power the Echo and Google Home devices.

I expect that the growth of chatbots will continue and we'll start seeing them used in a huge range of application and through a wide range of devices. As they improve, they'll be trusted with increasingly complex and important tasks and will completely revolutionize a lot of industries. Industries such as customer services are already changing, with chatbots on multiple banking and retail websites and phone systems.

# Language understanding

To be able to properly respond to someone, you need to understand what they are saying so you can build the correct response. This has improved a lot with the adoption of machine learning but is far from perfect.

One issue that can occur is that there are two intents with similar utterances, or with the same keyword in the utterances. When the user says a similar utterance, it matches both of the intents similarly and therefore can't choose which one to trigger. A chatbot with an intent with an utterance of `When is the football match?` and another intent with `Where is the football match?` is very likely to get confused and not be able to handle the request.

Another issue can be with spelling mistakes and typos. Lex currently seems to be OK with handling typos and spelling mistakes, but there have been quite a few times that these have caused issues.

As machine learning and language understanding improve, I expect to see these sorts of issues decrease.

# Working with spoken interactions

As with language understanding, being able to respond to a user's request means being able to understand what they said. With voice systems, this involves converting the spoken sound waves into text. Whilst this can work brilliantly if you happen to speak clearly with a neutral accent, there are often issues when people speak very quickly or with a strong accent.

When the text is generated from the users with a strong accent, it can often be misunderstood, and the text that is produced makes no sense. This then means that when it is passed into the language-understanding system, the speech can't be matched to an intent. This can be very frustrating for users with a strong accent who are unable to interact with these devices. This is a significant hurdle to overcome before voice-based chatbots become common in commercial applications.

# Improved device interaction

The continued increase of devices and systems that you can interact with through voice- and text-based conversation is key to the expansion of chatbots into our everyday lives. The great thing is that it's possible to install Alexa software onto a Raspberry Pi Zero, a $10 computer chip. This means that adding voice interaction to any device can be cheap and relatively simple. Alexa integration can already be seen in cars, smart mirrors, smart tables, and much more.

Another sector where I believe that chat interfaces are going to grow significantly is in wearables. Bluetooth hands-free systems are becoming smaller and more discrete and they could very easily integrate voice chat systems. At any point in your day, you could ask Alexa for the weather or the meetings for the day and get an instant response. This would overcome the security concerns that some people have about voice systems projecting their response for everyone in the room to hear.

Smart watches with built-in voice- and text-based chatbots provide another way that we will see chatbots integrated into our lives. The advantage of watches over earpieces is that they have screens, allowing the chatbot to display visual media or show the user the information, instead of having to say it all. Being able to glance at the weather is more convenient than having to listen to the weather forecast for the next five days when all you cared about was next Wednesday.

The last wearable that I can imagine using chatbots in the near future is smart glasses. Glasses similar to Google Glasses would allow you to receive visual information in the same way that a smart watch would, but you wouldn't even need to look down at your wrist. The addition of chatbots to an augmented reality system such as this could be very powerful.

The most powerful way the chatbots could be integrated into wearables would be an integration of multiple systems. Using an earpiece for a voice-based chat, but having a smart watch or smart glasses to display the visual information, would combine the best of both worlds.

# Connected devices

The second obstacle to overcome, before chatbots are commonplace, is the number of devices that can be connected to these smart home systems or remotely controlled solutions. You can currently get smart light switches, coffee makers, and even door locks that you can control through chat interfaces.

In the future, I expect that more and more devices will come out with a similar control system. I can imagine a washing machine that you can set and start by just talking to Alexa and eventually a kitchen where every device and appliance is speech-controlled. Imagine telling Alexa to turn the oven on to 180 degrees and to let you know when it gets to the right temperature, all while you sat watching TV, and then preparing a turkey and asking Alexa to open the oven so you can put it straight in. The oven could then weigh the turkey and set a reminder for 50 minutes before it will be ready to start preparing the roast potatoes.

As well as domestic appliances with integrated chatbots, I expect to see an increase in chatbots in businesses over the next 10-20 years. Bank tellers could become a screen with an animation of a person, powered by a voice-based chatbot. You could get your fresh meat and cheese from a chatbot that controls a robotic delicatessen. These could work in exactly the same way as current human workers, asking if that is a large enough piece of the brie wheel whilst holding the knife in position.

As well as commercial applications, I expect to see public service information begin to integrate chatbots. You arrive at the shopping center car park and want to find a particular store. All you need to do is to walk up to one of the information signs and ask where the shop is and it'll display the directions on a map, tell you how to get there, or even send the directions to your smart watch or smart glasses.

# Unique voice-based systems

To power the sorts of integrations and devices just mentioned, there needs to be a change in the way that voice-based chatbots are built. If you want to build a system that handles user speech, then your two main options are to build an Alexa Skill or a Google Home action. This is great for integrating into devices that already run these systems, but companies wouldn't want to run Alexa as your bank teller chatbot system.

There needs to be a change in the market with the move to being able to create custom voice-based chatbot systems that don't have to be run on Alexa or Google Home. This is currently possible through Amazon Lex, as it has been built to handle voice interaction, but I hope to see an increase in the range of systems that can do this.

# General Artificial Intelligence

A lot of the issues that exist with current chatbots will gradually be fixed, and their performance will increase incrementally, but the next large step forward will be the creation of **general AI**.

General AI is the concept where a single system can handle any request. This may sound not too far off with projects such as IBM Watson building a system that can dominate Jeopardy and other quiz games, but being able to answer simple questions is only part of the challenge.

The issues start when the system has to work out what other information it needs to fulfill the request and how to ask for that information. If someone asked you to find their class graduation photo, you would probably ask them what school they went to and what year they graduated in. You have used your knowledge about class photos to decide that you need to ask about school and year to accurately find their class photo. Our brains are extremely good at these sorts of tasks, but building an AI system that can work this out for every possible request, now or in the future, is a daunting task. Building an intent for every possible question just isn't possible so the system will need to gather what information it has on the topic, work out what else it needs to know to answer the question, and then ask for those pieces of data in a human way.

Another issue is with integrating into external systems. Throughout this book, we've used APIs to access data that is stored by a third party. To use these APIs, we had to have an API key, and, even then, we only had access to the data and functionality that we were given through the API. If we wanted to create a chatbot that did our weekly supermarket shop, had it delivered to our house, and paid for it, we'd need to get an API that allows us to do all of this. Creating an API like that is something I expect most supermarkets wouldn't dream of doing.

In my job, integrating into a client's existing system is a major hurdle to getting their chatbot functioning. Having a general AI system that has access to every API in the world is unrealistic, and, even then, there are systems that are not exposed through APIs.

# Improving people's opinions

One large hurdle to increased acceptance of chatbots is improving people's opinions of chatbots. When chatbots first came out, they were very limited in functionality, couldn't deal with many variations in utterance, and often proved to be more frustrating than useful. Modern chatbots have improved a lot, but there are a lot of older systems that are still very discouraging to use. Even modern chatbot systems have their limitation, as we've discussed earlier, and can still end up disappointing users with missed intents or misunderstood speech.

As the systems improve, better systems will have better user retention and the old systems will be replaced. I expect to see a continual improvement in people's opinions about chatbots. As systems like Alexa and Google Home become increasingly common in households, younger generations will grow up with chatbots and interacting with them will become second nature.

# Summary

This book has given us a practical introduction to chatbots through building increasingly complex Alexa Skills and Lex chatbots. We've learned about starting from a perfect conversation and creating flow diagrams to visualize the users' conversational path with a chatbot. Using these flow diagrams, we've built intents using utterances and slots that are handled in Lambdas.

We've improved the features and abilities of our chatbots through the use of S3 storage, DynamoDB databases, and external APIs. To improve the user experience, we also learned about using SSML to change how Alexa talks with our users, learned how to create cards to provide more visual information, and learned about search query slot types in Alexa for gathering wider ranges of slot values.

Finally, we've discussed a few great ways to build upon what we've already learned in this book and what we expect is in store for the future of chatbots.

# Appendix A

## Chapter 1

1. Intents, slots, and utterances
2. Any two from:
   - They are both Amazon services
   - They are both chatbots
   - They both use Natural Language Understanding/NLU/NLP
3. Any two from:
   - Alexa uses voice interaction, whereas Lex can be voice- or text-triggered
   - Alexa uses skills, whereas Lex can be applied to lots of applications
   - Lex can be triggered by other services, whereas Alexa only works on Alexa devices
4. You should start with a perfect conversation and build from there
5. **Tone of voice** is about the words and phrases that your chatbot uses and making sure that it suits the user
6. Missed utterances, external API errors, and errors in your code

## Chapter 2

1. Using the Lambda console on AWS, using Cloud9, on a local development setup
2. Amazon Web Services
3. No easy way to deploy or update Lambdas, and difficulty working on multiple machines or as part of a team
4. AWS-CLI, Bash/build scripts, Git, and GitHub/Bitbucket

# Chapter 3

1. `alexa-sdk`.
2. All three:
   - Copy the Lambda ARN into the **Skill Endpoint** default region
   - Copy the skill ARN into the Lambda code in the `exports.handler` function setup
   - Select **Alexa Skills Kit** as a trigger for the Lambda and copy the skill ARN into the setup
3. `s3.getObject()`.
4. You have to do `JSON.parse(data.body)` because the body of the reply is sent as a buffer, so it needs to be transformed into a usable JSON format.
5. Click the dropdown next to **Test** in the Lambda console and select **Configure test events**. You can then create a new test or modify an existing one.

# Chapter 4

1. An API is an **Application Programming Interface**, which allows the functionality of a program to be accessed from external sources.
2. `axios` is a promise-based library, whereas `HTTP` is callback-based.
3. Using `try/catch` and the `to` function method.
4. `this.attributes.colour = colour`.
5. Currently, only strings are allowed to be stored on session attributes.
6. You would use SSML to change the way that Alexa says something. This can be changing tone, emphasis, adding pauses, or a few other changes.

# Chapter 5

1. Yes, you can create the responses in the Lex console's **Intent Response** section
2. You need to wrap the name of the slot in curly brackets within the response
3. Lex can use one Lambda per intent, whereas Alexa handles all requests with a single Lambda
4. 5
5. `ElicitSlot, ElicitIntent, ConfirmIntent, Close, Delegate`
6. `` `S3.getObject() ``

# Chapter 6

1. A complex flow is made up of lots of different paths that the user can take, while a simple flow usually has a single path the user can take.
2. We can break the flow diagrams into sections. These sections can connect to other sections to create the total flow.
3. `ElicitSlot`, `Close`, `ElicitIntent`, `ConfirmIntent`, and `Delegate`.
4. The DynamoDB DocumentClient.

# Chapter 7

1. We want to integrate into other platforms and services to make it easier for our users to access our chatbots. Integrating with services that they already use makes accessing our chatbot much easier for them.
2. API Gateway and AWS Lambda.
3. Resources and methods.
4. We need to deploy the API onto a stage.
5. HTML file, JavaScript script, and a CSS file.
6. When a script file loads, it should check whether the DOM has fully loaded. If not, then it should wait for that to happen before running any functions that need to manipulate the DOM.

# Chapter 8

1. Cards are a great way to provide more information to the user without large blocks of text. Adding cards also allows you to provide buttons that give the user options for how to respond.
2. No, all of the attributes are optional, but a title and subtitle are recommended.
3. You'd use a **search query** slot type when there is a huge range of values that a user could enter. Creating a slot with everything would take too long and would still miss a lot of possible values.
4. Yes, but you can't populate a **search query** slot and another slot in the same utterance.
5. In Lex, the monitoring tab has a menu where it displays all of the missed intents. These can be looked through and added directly to an intent if needed.

# Appendix B

## Debugging

Trying to figure out why your code isn't working can be a very frustrating process and there can be loads of different sources of the issues. Throughout this book, we have three main sources of problems: Lambdas, Alexa Skill setup, and Lex setup.

## Debugging Alexa Skills

If your skill hasn't worked, then there are a few things that you need to check:

- You're using the correct utterances
- Your model has been saved and built
- Your endpoint is set correctly
- You've added Alexa as a trigger for your Lambda
- Your Lambda is working properly

## Check the utterances

If Alexa is replying with "Sorry, I don't know that one," make sure that you are saying or typing the correct phrase. It should be "Alexa, tell *your skill invocation your intent utterance*," so it might be, "Alexa, tell my skill hello" or "Alexa, ask car helper what car I should get." Check that you've correctly set your skill invocation and intent utterances. You can add more utterances to your intent so that it works with a larger variety of phrases.

You can also add console logs to your handlers to make sure that they are getting triggered when you expect them to.

## Save and build your model

Check that you've saved and built your model; the **Save Model** and **Build Model** buttons should be gray, not blue. There is no harm in re-saving and rebuilding your model to make sure that everything is up to date.

# Check your Endpoint

The last thing to check in the Alexa Skill Kit is that the **Endpoint** is correctly set. Make sure that there is a long ARN code in the **Default Region** box. If this isn't there, then open your Lambda console and find the Lambda that you want to be dealing with this skill. Copy the ARN number from the top right of the screen and paste it into the **Default Region** box in the Alexa Skill Kit. It should have the format `arn:aws:lambda:your-region:123456789012:function:your-lambda-name`.

# Added Alexa as a trigger for your Lambda

If your skill still isn't working, then there is probably a problem with your Lambda. In the Lambda editor, make sure that Alexa is on the design diagram exactly as shown next. If **Alexa Skill Kit** is not in that diagram, select it from the list of triggers on the left and follow the setup steps explained earlier in the chapter:

Alexa trigger

If the Alexa Skill Kit is shown but there is a message to complete configuration or something similar, then you need to do that. Click on the **Alexa Skill Kit** symbol and complete the configuration, as explained earlier in the chapter.

# Debugging Lex chatbots

As with Alexa skills, there are a few different places that can cause errors in your chatbot. Here are a few things you need to check:

- You are using the correct utterances

---

- Your intent has a text response or is triggering the correct Lambda
- Your intent has been saved and the chatbot built and deployed
- Your connected platform is properly configured (Facebook, Slack, API)
- Your Lambdas are working

# Check your utterances

If Lex is saying that it couldn't understand what you said, then it couldn't match your utterance to an intent. There are two ways this can happen: you don't have any sample utterances close enough to the utterance you used, or there are two sample utterances on different intents that match well. Having different intents with similar sample utterances can often cause issues.

# Check the intent response

Your intent may be getting hit, but it isn't returning a response. In the intent, scroll down to **Fulfillment** and make sure that either a Lambda is being invoked or you are replying with a text response. If you are invoking a Lambda, check the Lambda logs to see whether the Lambda is being run when you trigger that intent. If not, you may just need to save, build the chatbot, and deploy it again.

# Save intents, build, and deploy

If all of your sample utterances and fulfillments are correct, then you should make sure every intent is saved, build your chatbot, and deploy it to the same alias as before. It is very easy to forget this step and wonder why all of your changes haven't made any difference.

# Check your connected platform

If you are trying to connect your chatbot to a platform such as Facebook, Slack, or your API, make sure that they are set up properly. If you can successfully test your chatbot in the Lex console, then go back through the setup processes for the platform and make sure that you haven't missed a step.

# Check your Lambdas are working

Use the Lambda debugging tips to ensure that your Lambdas are responding with the correct responses.

# Debugging Lambdas

If you have found that the problem is not with your Alexa skill or Lex chatbot, there might be a problem with your Lambda. Before you start changing things in your code, it is often a good idea to create a test in the Lambda console. This should represent the request that is being sent by Alexa or Lex. Use this test to see whether it is your Lambda that is at fault or it works as expected.

If your test is unsuccessful, look in the logs for the error messages. This can often point you to the root of the problem.

Here are some things to check when trying to debug a Lambda:

- Your Lambda has all of the required packages installed
- Your permissions are correct
- All of your variables are correctly defined
- Your Lambda code is correct
- Everything your Lambda calls is working

# Install all of the required packages

If your Lambda isn't working, you need to check that all the packages are installed. Go to your `Lambdas` folder and navigate to your problem Lambda. In it, there should be an `archive.zip` zipped file. If there isn't, run the build script again and an `archive.zip` file should appear – your Lambda should now work.

If there is an `archive.zip` file, open it and see what it contains. There should be an `index.js` file, a `package.json` or `package-lock.json` file, and a `node_modules` folder. If any of these things are missing, then rerun the build script and make sure that it succeeds.

If all of that is correct, then check inside `package.json` or `package-lock.json` that there are dependencies for all of the packages that you are requiring in your Lambda code. Check that there is also a folder for each of the packages inside `node_modules`. If there isn't, you will need to run `npm install --save *PACKAGE-NAME*` to add it to the `package.json` file.

# Check your permissions

Go into your Lambda, scroll down to the **Execution role**, and see which role you have selected. Now, go to the **IAM** service and select the role that you have used. Look through the policies that you have added to that role and make sure that you have all the permissions that you need. Add any policies that you need for the role.

# Correct your Lambda code

You also need to check that the code in your Lambda is correct. As your Lambdas become more complex, it becomes harder to get them working the first time. Run the tests that you've created, and look for the error message.

If you don't know what the error message means or how to fix it, search online as there will have been other people who have encountered this error before. Make sure you read the replies on how to fix the error and understand why that solution works before using it in your code. It helps you become a better developer and allows you to fix it if there is an error with it in the future.

If the bug isn't obvious from the error message, you can use `console.log('Some information')` to log out whenever your code gets to each stage. Use this to work out how far your code is getting and what values are available at that point. It can often be that variables or responses from other services are not in the format that you expected them to be in. Being able to see all of your data just before the error is really useful in finding out why your code isn't working.

# Check external services

When working with external services, there is always the possibility that those services stop working or change their response. Every time you deal with an external service, you should handle it, if it is returning an error. If the services appear to be working but your code is not working, then `console.log` out the response to check the format.

# Other Books You May Enjoy

If you enjoyed this book, you may be interested in these other books by Packt:

**Hands-On Chatbots and Conversational UI Development**
Srini Janarthanam

ISBN: 978-1-78829-466-9

- Design the flow of conversation between the user and the chatbot
- Create Task model chatbots for implementing tasks such as ordering food
- Get new toolkits and services in the chatbot ecosystem
- Integrate third-party information APIs to build interesting chatbots
- Find out how to deploy chatbots on messaging platforms
- Build a chatbot using MS Bot Framework
- See how to tweet, listen to tweets, and respond using a chatbot on Twitter
- Publish chatbots on Google Assistant and Amazon Alexa

**Voice User Interface Projects**
Henry Lee

ISBN: 978-1-78847-335-4

- Understand NLP platforms with machine learning
- Exploit best practices and user experiences in creating VUI
- Build voice-enabled chatbots
- Host, secure, and test in a cloud platform
- Create voice-enabled applications for personal digital assistant devices
- Develop a virtual assistant for cars

# Leave a review – let other readers know what you think

Please share your thoughts on this book with others by leaving a review on the site that you bought it from. If you purchased the book from Amazon, please leave us an honest review on this book's Amazon page. This is vital so that other potential readers can see and use your unbiased opinion to make purchasing decisions, we can understand what our customers think about our products, and our authors can see your feedback on the title that they have worked with Packt to create. It will only take a few minutes of your time, but is valuable to other potential customers, our authors, and Packt. Thank you!

# Index